America's Government

How it Works, its Strengths, its Weaknesses, its Preservation

By

Harley Ruft

Copyright 2018, Harley Ruft

All rights reserved. Printed in the United States of America.

This publication is protected by Copyright and permission
should be obtained from the author prior to any prohibited
reproduction, storage in a retrieval system, or transmission in
any form by any means, electronic, mechanical, photocopying,
and recording or likewise.   For information regarding
permission(s), write to the author through the publisher.

Dedicated to my beloved wife, Marilyn

Preface

One of the glaring deficiencies of America's democracy is the lack of participation on the part of its citizenry. Less than fifty percent of eligible voters participate in hotly contested presidential elections and it is down hill from there for lesser elections. Billion dollar school budgets often are approved by less than ten percent of the eligible voters. Why does this condition exist? There are as many reasons as there are people who do not vote, but a contributing factor is many Americans do not know enough about their government to realize the importance and necessity of their participation. Election ballots typically contain a dozen or more candidates and several propositions. It takes effort on the part of voters to know enough about the candidates and issues to vote intelligently. It is the purpose of his book to describe how American's government works. Its objective is increased citizen participation and better government.

This book is written for use in high school civics programs. Voting starts at 18 years old and young people need to start to vote as soon as they reach the age of eligibility. They should establish a strategy for participation. Some will want to run for office. This short book will give young people the information about their government that they need to understand how the system works and what their role should be. This book is also suitable as a guide for people seeking citizenship and older Americans who want to increase their understanding of America's government and its politics.

This book is written from the perspective of a person who has had active participation as a committee person in one of America's two major political parties for more than 40 years. It is an insider's chronicle of how the system works, where there are strengths, where there are weaknesses, and some suggestions (Author's Commentary) on how to fix some of our systemic problems. This book is an attempt on the part of a person at end of life to pass on decades of learning of how American politics work and how future generations can keep America's democracy intact and healthy.

What's in this book? We start with discussing the pros and cons of democracy as an option for any society. Then we describe America's democracy: our Constitution, our political parties, the workings of our government at all levels. Then we get into the workings of our political parties, becoming a candidate for office, and we conclude with a discussion of every person's responsibility in maintaining a democracy. Each chapter is followed by questions and a limited list of books related to the subject of each chapter. This book is a must for all students. They are the ones who need to know how America's government works if it is to be preserved.

Regards,
HR

Table of Contents

<u>Chapter</u>

Chapter 1

What is a Democracy?

I am not an anthropologist, so I cannot present facts about the origin of structured societies, but we all know that early civilizations had leaders who usually had complete control over "subjects." In the caveman era, the leader of a collection of people may have been the biggest, strongest, or smartest of the group. Whenever people live in close proximity, it is a natural instinct for these people to band together to address tasks of mutual benefit like protection. We are animals as well as humans, and we follow animal instincts with regard to formation of groups with a leader. Many animals mate for life. Many animal species form groups (prides, gaggles, herds, etc.). Nature dictates that these basic elements have leaders. The male is the leader in many animal families. He protects the family and in some cases, is a major supplier of food. Groups of animals band together, usually for protection. A herd of gazelle has a better survival chance than individual families wondering in the bush. It is more likely that one of the gazelles in a herd will sense a predator and warn the others so that they can boogie on out of there. So it is nature's way that the family is the basic unit in a society. It is natural for families to band together into a unit of society, and it is natural for a leader to evolve to guide the larger unit. Thus, forming a society is a natural instinct and the orderly societies can form a civilization. Whales may be the best example of a civilization. Whales are found in all oceans of the world. There are many different species and each species lives together, but they coexist in a common ocean and generally get along. Their civilization has survived for thousands of years. I suspect that sharks have a similar civilization. Whales and sharks are "stronger" than many marine species and that probably is a factor in the survivability of a society. Our point here is that it is a natural thing for people to live with the family as the basic unit, for families to form larger societal units, and that there be some type of leadership for the larger societal unit. A civilization is created when the larger societal units learn to

9

live together. The better the families get along in these societies, the higher the civilization. Our definition of a civilization is people living in a harmony created by rules and regulations -- the greater the order, the higher the level of civilization.

Autocratic Societies

Kings, queens, emperors, dictators have been in charge of civilizations for as long as there has been recorded history. Sometime in the evolution of groups with "leaders" these leaders decided that being a leader of a group is a good gig. They decided to keep the job and pass it on to their offspring. This was the beginning of kings and queens. This societal system would work if the grand fubar was extremely wise, extremely likeable, extremely compassionate, and had children that were the same and got along great. We all know that most autocratic societies no longer exist because messianic leaders seldom carry through generations.

The Catholic Church is an example of an autocratic society that so far has passed the test of time. Probably, the reason for this is that it is not a family thing. The Pope is the absolute leader of the clergy and Catholics believe that anything that the Pope asks them to do is sanctioned by God. Popes, historically, have been good guys for the most part and they are not born into the job. They are selected as the most capable by their peers to lead the Catholic Church. I have never met a Pope, but for the 30 years that Pope John Paul II has been in charge, he epitomized what a leader should be; generous, charismatic, compassionate, wise, and utterly holy. I believe that miracles will be performed in his name and he will become a saint.

Unfortunately, in my lifetime, I have witnessed kings and queens in Europe diminished in power and prestige. Many royal families do not live in a manner that makes constituents revere them and want them to be in actual charge of running their society. They are, for the most part, relegated to ceremonial status and serve to promote tourism. Some, like Queen Elizabeth of the UK, serve as examples of proper social behavior and etiquette. She acts like a queen and inspires her "subjects" to behave in a civil manner. On the other hand, my lifetime has witnessed the absolute crime to humanity that is Fidel Castro. For forty years he has kept millions of Cubans in abject poverty, isolated from the rest of the world. He maintains his status by controlling the military and annihilating all who challenge his power. I suspect that there is a special place in Hell for him, Stalin, Napoleon, Mao Tse Tung and the rest of the despots who destroyed their civilizations.

Early Democracies

The word "democracy" is derived from the Greek "democrat" which means to share with people. There were societies that were governed by consensus in ancient times. The Bible recounts times when the Jews did not have a king and were ruled by some sort of consensus system. They were a democracy. The people participated in their destiny. People shared in decisions on the society. A democracy requires that members of the society have a way to express their wants and that they also participate in deciding laws, regulations, and direction.

Unfortunately, there have not been many significant democracies that have survived the test of time. China has never had one; India never tried it until they copied the colonial England system. Japan had emperors and war lords until after World War II. Russia was ruled by czars up until the twentieth century. England's parliament system was not a democracy until the people diminished the power of the monarchy. Thus, it may be that the USA's "democracy" is one of the oldest surviving within large countries. The concept of having people contribute to their society's direction is sound and desirable. It is a basic human instinct to have a say in things that affect your well being. In the basic unit of society, the family, wives want a say in where and how they live, as do husbands. The reality of the situation, however, is impasse. The wife wants granite countertops in the kitchen and the husband wants laminate. He wants a Pontiac Vibe; she wants a Dodge Viper. Democracies need a mechanism to arbitrate opposing opinions. In the family unit, the wife usually recalls her childhood "princess" status to override husband wishes. Many democracies lack this deciding function, and end up in stalemate status where nothing gets done and the people's situation degrades. This situation existed in 2008 in Iraq. Sectarian factions could not agree on the country's direction so they have no direction. Their infrastructure is in shambles and the people lack basic services. Thus, this is the classic cause for the failure of democracies. There is no way to force arbitration of disputes.

In summary, a democracy is a form of government which allows people a say in what the government does. Democracies have been around for thousands of years, but only about a third of the world's people live in one. Is it the best form of government for the USA? Probably.

Strengths of America's Democracy

As I write this, Egypt has just encountered a revolution that deposed their dictator after 30 plus years in power. More than 40 percent of their eighty million people exist on less than two US dollars a day. There were so many people in desperate straits that they had nothing to lose by revolting. In the words of one of the revolutionaries, "many, many people eat from the trash." Egypt had a "democracy;" they had an elected president and a parliament. However, opposition parties to the presidents' were outlawed, so elections were meaningless. The president (dictator) was the only person "running." There are many "democracies" on our planet that are a sham. They do not really allow citizens to participate; they do not allow opposing parties; they do not allow freedom of speech, and the most glaring defect in Middle East "democracies" is freedom of religion. I have an Egyptian friend who became a Christian. He told me that he could be killed if he ever returned to Egypt by those who promote the country as a theocracy. Theocracies are incommensurate with democracy.

America's constitution solves the theocracy problem. In fact, freedom of religion is one of the most significant attributes of America's democracy. America's democracy has always allowed for opposing opinions on how to run the country with our two-party system. The two-party system is not guaranteed by the Constitution, but it has evolved to the point where it may be he model for all democracies. All political parties are allowed, but the voting public has opted (over 200 years) to have just two sides to almost every issue. Occasionally our two parties even agree – like when we declare wars.

Another great feature of our democracy is civilian control of the military. This is also not guaranteed by the Constitution, but we all know that whoever controls the "means of force" also controls the populace. Countless nations on our planet are ruled by the military. Egypt now is. It has been the practice since World War II to have the military report to the Secretary of Defense who has been a civilian for the past 60 years or so. This allows America's president the option to fire any military leader who tends to want to become president by force. Several firings of military leaders usually occur in each administration.

True freedom of the press is another hallmark of America's democracy. The press, film, and electronic media are the watchdogs of our democracy. If an elected official commits an impropriety it soon becomes common knowledge and action occurs. Within the past year or two, a governor, a comptroller, two House Representatives, a state senate majority leader, and quite a number of lesser elected officials have been pushed out of office because of revelations brought to light in our press. Public disclosure of stupid, illegal, and unethical actions on the part of elected officials usually leads to indictments or resignations. This certainly helps to clean up our leadership.

A unique strength of America's democracy is the amalgamation of people with differing birth circumstances: ethnicity, country of origin, customs, and proclivities. Many of the people who resided in the American colonies when the

Constitution and the USA was formed were there because of persecutions or economic biases in their countries of origin. The Puritans came to northeastern America because of religious persecution in England. The Catholics came to Maryland for the same reason. Some came from other countries to find fortune in a "new" environment. The people who wrote the Constitution came from many places, many backgrounds, and they crafted the document to allow non-indigenous citizens to run for most elected offices. America is a country formed by immigrants to be friendly to immigrants and to have citizens from every other country and every other background – a strength that most other countries do not have. Unfortunately, the founders of the United States did not treat the people who owned the country, the Native Americans, very kindly. They are finally getting some remuneration in the form of gambling casinos on "their property," but the problem of the stronger taking over the land of the weaker is something that cannot be solved by political systems. This tendency is rooted in the animal instincts that are part of being human. People have an animal instinct to survive. People have an animal instinct to carve out their own territory. Political systems must deal with these. Borders are the current attempt to deal with this aspect of human nature. All civilizations, all nations have to deal with this issue. America has another significant strength in this regard: we have significant water boundaries for most of the country. This minimizes the boundary disputes that America must deal with. Islands are always a problem and countries will be vying for them as long as they exist. America still does not know what to do about Puerto Rico, Guam, and some others. Hawaii took decades to resolve.

The Weakness of America's Democracy

Gridlock is probably the most significant weakness of any participatory government. People cannot agree on a path forward so no motion occurs. This is not usually a problem in America because we tend to elect enough pro and con legislatures to keep the President or legislative bodies in check. Lopsided party participation in America's cities, however, has essentially destroyed most US cities as a place to live. One political party controls the cities and the corruption that comes with lack of significant opposition destroys that entity.

Another significant problem with America's democracy was legislation in the 1960's allowing public employees to form unions. In 2011, public employees at almost every level have unions that usurp control of services and the common good. The citizens of the United States have ceded control of schools, trash collection, road maintenance, public health facilities, hospitals – everything that relates to needs for the common good are controlled by unions that have enrichment of their leaders and members as their goal. Unions were started to end employer abuses, but they gravitated into "member business" that have produced wage and benefit increases that are incommensurate with market rates. They need to go back to their original intent – prevent employer abuse/injustice on the part of employers. Pay and benefits for all jobs should be an individual thing – each person needs to negotiate his or her raise. Groups do not deserve raises. There are many other encroachments on the fundamentals offered citizens by our Constitution and more specifics will be noted in subsequent chapters. In 2011, unnecessary regulations and mandates from lawmakers at every level have made it next to impossible to form a business and employ people. This has brought a lack of jobs problem that rivals the great depression of the 1930's

Author's Commentary

We must return control of what the government does, its services, to citizens. Citizens have lost their say in capital projects, government services, even going to war. Establishing citizenship requirements and enforcement of borders will restore "requirements of citizenship," a necessary part of a democracy. Citizen participation in our political system, the goal of this book, will address all other weaknesses in our democracy. America's democracy is critically ill because of lack of participation. Too many people do not vote. Too may people fail to share their talents in running the country. Too many Americans let "someone else do it."

Questions

1. What is a democracy?
2. Describe an early democracy.
3. What is civilization and how does government affect it?
4. List 3 advantages and 3 disadvantages of a monarchy.
5. What is a dictatorship?
6. What form of government does The Peoples Republic of China have?
7. What is a theocracy? Name one.
8. What is a citizen's role in a democracy?
9. How does America's constitution fit into its democracy?
10. List four countries currently ruled by dictators.

Related Reading

1. Fleming, Daniel E., <u>Democracy's Ancient Ancestors:</u> Mari and Early Collective Governance, 2004.

2. Pirenne, Henri, <u>Early Democracies in the Low Countries:</u> Urban Society and Political Conflict in the Middle Ages and Renaissance, 1971.

3. Robinson, Eric W., <u>The First Democracies:</u> Early Popular Government Outside Athens,   1997.

4. Guedalla, Phillip, <u>The Partition of Europe, A Textbook of European History</u>, 2009.

5. Schmitt, Carl, <u>Dictatorship</u>, 2011.

Chapter 2

America's Democracy

Some civics authorities claim that a true democracy requires three attributes: (1) All citizens have access to elected office (2) all citizens have defined freedoms (3) there are requirements for citizenship.

America's democracy started with the Declaration of Independence wherein a group of people with abilities that differentiated them from ordinary citizens, took it upon themselves to draft a document that stated America was going to become independent of England. King George did not accept this news in a friendly manner, and the war of independence was the result. America won the war and the confederation of states that constituted America at that time, decided it was appropriate to establish rules for the entire group – the Confederation of States.

The group of leaders from the states was called the Continental Congress. They met in Independence Hall in Philadelphia in 1787 to establish a constitution or set of rules for the American democracy. Prior to the war of independence, the states that made up America had no overarching government control. Britain (King George) ruled America prior to the War of Independence (1775 – 1783). They could not tax as a nation and states had no ruling powers. The Constitution was written by Governor Morris of New York. The purpose of the document is stated in the preamble:

> "We the people of the United States, in order to
> form a more perfect union, establish justice, ensure
> domestic tranquility, provide for the common defense,
> promote the general welfare and secure the blessings
> of liberty to ourselves and our posterity do ordain
> and establish this Constitution of the United States
> of America."

The plan was to have three branches in this centralized government: executive, legislative, judicial. George Washington was chosen by the group to be President, the leader of the executive branch of the government. The legislative branch of the government was described in Article 1, and the document contains seven articles dealing with different functions.

ARTICLE I

Section 1: This section creates a congress with a Senate and a House of Representatives.

Section 2: This section sets forth the rules for the House of Representatives:

- ✓ Members shall be chosen every second year
- ✓ Must be 25 years of age and a citizen for seven years and an inhabitant of the United States at the time of election
- ✓ The number of representatives in a state is determined by their populations – basically one representative per each 300,000 citizens
- ✓ Each state shall have at least one
- ✓ Vacancies are to be filled by state elections
- ✓ The House will chose its speaker and other officers
- ✓ The House shall have power to impeach

Section 3: This section establishes the senate composed of two senators from each state:

- ✓ Senator terms shall be 6 years
- ✓ Each senator has one vote
- ✓ State executives can fill vacancies until the next election

- ✓ Candidates must be 30 years of age, nine years a citizen, and reside in the state where elected
- ✓ The vice president of the United States shall be the president of the Senate
- ✓ The Senate will try all impeachments
- ✓ A 2/3 majority is needed for impeachment

Section 4: This section establishes when states will hold elections for members of congress – whenever they want and that congress shall assemble at least once a year.

Section 5: This section states that a simple majority in each house shall constitute a quorum and states that votes of members should be made public (if one-fifth agree) and a journal shall be kept of proceedings unless they are secret for security reasons. Also, the house cannot adjourn for more than three days or meet elsewhere.

Section 6: The senators and representatives will be compensated for their services by the treasurer of the United States and they cannot be officers (President, Vice President, etc.) and still keep their senate or house seats.

Section 7: The House of Representatives is responsible for bills raising revenue and bills must have been passed by both houses and approved by the president before they become the law of the United States. If a bill is not approved by the president, it will require a 2/3 majority of both houses to override the president's veto. If a bill is approved by both houses and is sent to the president, it becomes law if he does not act on it in 10 days.

Section 8: This section enumerates the powers of Congress pertaining to taxation, mail service, military service, waging war, printing money, etc. – all laws necessary and proper for executing the foregoing powers.

Section 9: The first part states that Congress shall not deny immigration that the states think proper to admit. Congress shall not tax articles exported from any state. A financial statement of the treasury shall be periodically published. There shall be no titles of nobility granted by the US, or accepted and presented, or title from a foreign state.

Section 10: No state shall enter into treaties with foreign powers, impose tariffs, or have their own army.

ARTICLE II

Section 1: The executive power of the United States shall be vested in a president elected for a 4-year term with a vice-president with the same term. The president must be a citizen of the United States for at least 14 years and a US resident. The vice-president will take over as president if the president cannot complete his term for a reason like sickness or heath. The president shall receive a salary which will not change during his or her term.

The president is to be elected by electors from each state and the number from each state shall be equal to the number of congressmen and senators from that state. The electors cannot be elected federal officials. The details of the election process used by the electors has evolved from that of making deals on the constitution such that they meet after the popular election and cast their vote for whoever won the popular election in their state.

Section 2: The President shall be Commander-in-Chief of the US military, shall have the power to grant pardons, shall make treaties (if 2/3 of senators approve), and shall appoint ministers and ambassadors and judges to the Supreme Court.

Section 3: The president shall periodically inform Congress of the state of the union and make recommendations to Congress for changes and projects that are deemed necessary.

Section 4:   The president, vice-president and civil officers can be impeached for misdeeds.

ARTICLE III

Section 1: The Supreme Court is the seat of the country's judicial power along with its lower courts.

Section 2: The judicial power shall extend to all cases between citizens, states, treaties, and crimes. Crime shall be judged in the states where they are committed and trial shall be by jury, except impeachment.

Section 3: This section defines treason as warring against the USA or aiding enemies.

ARTICLE IV

Section 1: "Full faith and credit shall be given in each state to the public acts, records, and judicial proceedings of every other state." This means states need to recognize each other.

Section 2: Citizens of one state should have the same rights as citizens in other states, and people committing crimes in one state and fleeing to another shall be returned to the state where the crime was committed.

Section 3: New states can be admitted to the USA, but new states cannot be created out of existing states.

Section 4: The US shall guarantee all states a republican form of government and protect each state from invasion.

ARTICLE V

The Constitution can be amended by 2/3 of both houses of Congress or by 2/3 of the states.

ARTICLE VI

The Constitution and laws made to it are the supreme law of the land and all judges must adhere to these laws. No religious test shall ever be required as a qualification for any office of public trust.

ARTICLE VII

This section states that the ratification of the Constitution by the nine existing states shall be sufficient to establish this Constitution as the law of the land and the document is signed by representatives from eleven states.

Summary

The Constitution of the United States set forth an organization and operating plan that was fairly simple and understandable. There are three branches: the executive, legislative, and judicial. The document outlined the operating responsibilities, details, and duties of each branch. It was ratified by enough states for adoption, but the states and congress wanted the ability to add amendments to the Constitution as needs arose. To that end, in 1789, Congress sent 12 amendments to state legislatures to get their approval to become amendments to the Constitution. Ten of the 12 amendments were approved and they became what are now known as the Bill of Rights. Other amendments followed, but every US citizen has a stake in the Bill of Rights since it defines the freedoms that our "democracy" will provide.

BILL OF RIGHTS

Amendment I - Congress shall make no law that:

1. establishes a religion
2. limits free speech or press

3.   limits the right of peaceable assembly
4.   limits the right of people to petition the
        government to redress grievances

Amendment II – The US government shall allow states to maintain a militia and all citizens the right to bear arms.

Amendment III – No soldier in the time of peace shall be quartered in a house without the consent of the owner; and only in a lawful manner in time of war.

Amendment IV – The government cannot search people, their houses, papers, and possessions without a proper and justifiable court warrant.

Amendment V – A grand jury indictment is necessary for capital or otherwise "infamous" crime; also, a person cannot be tried twice for the same crime; also, no person shall be compelled in a trial to be a witness against himself, nor to be deprived of life, liberty or property without due process of law; nor shall private property be taken for public use without just compensation.

Amendment VI – Citizens accused of a crime shall be guaranteed a speedy and public trial by an impartial jury of the state wherein the crime was committed. The accused shall be informed of the nature of the accusation, confronted with witnesses against him, and have the right to obtain witnesses in his favor and a counsel for his defense.

Amendment VII – In suits at common law, the right of trial by jury shall be preserved, and no fact tried by a jury shall be otherwise re-examined in an US court, than according to the rules of the common law.

Amendment VIII – Excessive bail shall not be required, nor excessive fines imposed, nor cruel and unusual punishment inflected.

Amendment IX – The enumeration in the Constitution of certain rights shall not be construed to deny or disparage others retained by the people.

Amendment X – The powers not delegated to the United States by the Constitution, nor prohibited by it to the states, are reserved to the states respectively or to the people.

Summary

There were 22 amendments to the Constitution in 2009, but most of those passed since the Bill of Rights deal with details surrounding implementation of the original Constitution and Bill of Rights.

Strengths of America's Constitution

A fundamental strength of America's Constitution is its simplicity. In 2010 in the USA most legal documents are written (in the smallest font allowable) in legalize with the intent that it can only be interpreted by a lawyer. America's tax law is a perfect example. It is so unintelligible that most citizens have to hire someone to do their taxes.

Another significant strength is the ability of amendment. This allows our "rules" to be altered as times change. A related strength is the difficulty of amending the Constitution. Amendments require an "approval" vote by two-thirds of the members of both houses of congress as well as "approval" votes from two-thirds of the states. This is a very significant requirement and thus the constitution will never be amended for trivial reasons or without overwhelming popular support. This is the way it should be.

Weaknesses of Our Constitution

As we will point out in subsequent chapters, a critical weakness of America's Constitution is that it does not address election details. Where do candidates for office come from?

Where does one apply for the presidency? How do competing factions sponsor candidates for office? Of course, political parties supply candidates for office and there are government functions in place to supervise elections, but there are no rules or even guidelines on the operation of political parties. They can operate any way that they want. There could be a political party with the singular goal of legalizing heroin use and this is acceptable. There could be a political party open only to billionaires with a goal of "buying" the presidency and thus gaining significant control of America's populace. There simply are no rules or guidelines pertaining to endorsing candidates for elected positions. How does an average American get his or her name on a ballot for election? The Constitution skips this basic requirement of a democracy: all citizens can have access to elected office.

The similar critical flaw in the Constitution is assumed power of the Supreme Court to make laws. They can and have usurped the will of the people and the constitution to make laws. The death penalty is a "law," but it is clearly prohibited by our constitution under the "cruel and inhumane punishment" clause. Abortion on demand is prohibited by Section II of 'Amendment XIV: "nor shall any state deprive any person of life, liberty, or property without due process of law." Forceps and head crunching implements are hardly "due process of law." The Supreme Court violated the Constitution and made murder permissible and because there is nothing in the Constitution to allow the citizens to override a Supreme Court decision that is believed by all of its of its citizens to be unconstitutional.

Author's Commentary

America's democracy is based upon a relatively simple constitution and it is a reasonable democracy on paper because it guarantees key freedoms. The problem that has evolved is that we have had more than 200 years of federal and state laws crafted since the Constitution that dither with our rights and, in many cases, directly violate the Constitution. America's elected leaders need to re-read the Constitution and Bill of Rights on a quarterly basis. Americans should have the constitution as their computer screen saver. It is quite a good work and it is also the basis for the continual improvement of our democracy. We need to restore its intent – a government that citizens can participate in, a government that respects the rights and freedoms of its citizens. We need the constitution altered to prohibit supreme court decisions that are counter to our constitution based upon popular interpretation – what the majority of its citizens believe to be its meaning.

Questions

1. List three requirements of a democracy.
2. Who wrote America's Constitution?
3. What constitutes congress?
4. What constitutes a district with a representative to the House of Representative?
5. What constitutes a district for a U.S. senator?
6. What are the duties of the President?
7. What are the duties of the Vice-President?
8. What are the requirements for office for: President? Vice-President? Senator? Representative? Federal Judge?
9. What is impeachment?
10. What does it take to impeach a President, Vice-President, Senator, Representative?
11. What are the constitutional terms of office for President, Vice-President, Senator, Representative, federal judge, Supreme Court judge?
12. What constitutes a quorum in the Senate? In the House?
13. What limits does the constitution put on the powers of states?
14. What is the "Bill of Rights?"
15. What document provides the right to a jury trial? Illegal search? Excessive bail? Cruel and unusual punishment?
16. What part of the constitution or Bill of Rights guarantees private ownership of property?
17. What document allows adding more states to the USA?

18.   What founding document guarantees freedom of
        religion?
19.   What does the constitution say about taxation of its
        citizens?

Related Reading

1.   Amar, Akhel Reed, America's Constitution: A
        Biography, 2008
2.   Franklin, Benjamin, Declaration of Independence,
        Constitution of the United States of America, Bill of
        Rights and Constitutional Amendments, 2010

3.   Fink, Sam, The Constitution of the United States of
        America, 2010

4.   Lane, Eric and Oreskes, Michael, The Genius of
        America: How the Constitution Saved Our Country
        and How it Can Again, 2007

5.   The Constitution of the United States

Chapter 3

Alternates to America's Democracy

Is a democracy the best form of government for the United States? The founding fathers thought so and they established a constitution to spell out how that democracy should be run. However, in 2010, the United States of America is in an untenable global position. After 200+ years of facing wars and economic challenges, America has been "defeated" by foreign debt. America could be foreclosed on and would no longer exist as a nation. We will be the victims of a hostile takeover, and unintentional merger. Maybe the founding fathers should have considered another form of government. Let's explore some options.

Monarchy:

When the United States was formed, there were still lots of monarchies around. Americans were revolting England's monarchy (King George), but France, Spain, Portugal – lots of countries were also ruled by kings and queens. Many were absolute leaders; most or the monarchs had advisors to guide them in decisions, but when a reigning king or queen made a pronouncement, it was in essence a law. The citizens were expected to obey or face prison or whatever penalty the monarch wanted to impose. John the Baptist was beheaded at the request of one of King Herod's dancing girls. The most "forbidden" word in the English language is reported to be an acronym for an edict by a medieval monarch after his country's population was decimated by a plague and he wanted his country rebuilt: "Fornicate under command of the king."

Kings and queens ordered wars that killed thousands, even hundreds of thousands for sometimes trivial reasons. After the American Revolution, a number of countries ruled by monarchs initiated systems to give the citizens some say in their government. England's monarchy evolved into a "democracy" with the king or queen having mostly ceremonial duties. However, in England, the monarch "on paper" still controls the country. The chief executive of the United Kingdom is the Prime Minister. The Prime Minister is selected by the members of Parliament and they can oust the Prime Minister if they want with a no-confidence vote. He or she must dissolve Parliament and call for new elections of Members of Parliament (MP). The country is divided into constituencies which consist of a fixed number of citizens like 60,000 in a contiguous locale. They are analogous to the US House of Representatives districts. England has two major political parties (Labor and Conservative) and the parties decide on who the candidates will be for every elected post in the same way as it is done in the US. A huge difference mentioned previously is that an MP candidate cannot spend more than a fixed (small) amount on a campaign. The Conservative Party started as the "land owner's party." The Labor Party started as the party of the worker peasants. They have a significant third party, the Liberal Party, which can at times determine elections of leaders of Parliament.

However, Parliament and the Prime Minister serve at the pleasure of the reigning monarch. The monarch can dissolve Parliament and call for new elections. No monarchs have done this in the last century. Members of Parliament have variable terms in office based upon when prime ministers change, but all are supposed to be in place no longer than five years without reelection. England is bicameral; Parliament consists of two houses, the House of Lords and the House of Commons. The House of Lords consists of "titled" aristocrats (lords, dukes, etc.) plus some non-titled commoners who have made significant contributions to England. Members of the House of Lords number about 100 and they do not have the power of the House of Commons. England does not have a constitution to serve as the basis for their democracy. They are a much older society than the US and England's "Common Law" which evolved over a thousand years or so serves as the basis of their society.

Many "democracies" in the world, probably most democracies, have opted for this system of government. Why didn't our founding fathers? After America successfully beat off the British, there was a movement among some leaders of the Confederation of States to make George Washington the king of the United States and for America to become a monarchy. We know that this did not come about, but they did not choose a parliamentary form of government probably because they wanted the chief executive directly elected by the citizenry rather than by these elected representatives. Was this the right choice? The jury may still be out. However, when one objectively observes the shenanigans that take place in selecting leaders in our House and Senate, it appears to be the right choice.

History has shown that monarchies work just fine as long as you have a good monarch. There is an incredible advantage in having an absolute leader. He or she can order things done. He or she can build pyramids, incredible palaces, phenomenal parks and gardens, etc. Things can get done. Democracies require a consensus to do anything and sometimes a consensus can never be arrived at so things do not get done. In any case, monarchies have gone the way of roll film. There are not many absolute monarchies left except in small countries that have opted not to participate in the "global economy." Many former monarchies even lost their identifying currencies. Nineteen former monarchies in Europe now use a common currency. The ubiquitous "Euro."

A fundamental property of monarchies is that most were intended to be passed from one generation to the next. A quirk of nature is that one's progeny may be dissimilar. Sometimes offspring are not like their parents (it happens) and a good king or queen may produce a first in line offspring without the necessary credentials to run a country. Royals seem to be fraught with human (and damaging) frailties. Most monarchies have weaned power from their royals and they now serve in ceremonial roles often aimed at increasing the country's tourist industry. So, kings and queens are not considered viable government options by many countries in the world because of "bad" experiences in the past.

Communism

We mentioned earlier that this is one of the oldest forms of governing a society. The Catholic Church was a communal society in its early days. They pooled their resources and each was given what they needed from the common treasury and food source: from each according to his or her abilities and to each according to his or her needs. Everybody gets the same. The Catholic Church still has all of their assets in a common "treasury" under control of Church leaders, but members and clergy are on their own for sustenance/daily needs. There are many religious orders that have operated successfully for centuries as communal societies, but history has shown that these kinds of societies offer a spartan existence that does not appeal to many. It works best with individuals who devote their lives to God and have no desire for earthly wealth or possessions. So, if you are like some people who prefer a fine house, a great automobile, great food and drink, travel, and every amenity to going to daily mass, baking bread, eating just soup and bread, praying for hours every day, and sleeping on a hard bed in a Spartan room, then you would not want a community form of government controlling your life.

It took about seventy years, but the largest communist society the world has ever known, the USSR, eventually crumbled. There are a number of fundamental flaws in the communist theory of government. The most significant is "from each according to his or her abilities and to each according to his or her needs." Why should I work my butt off when I will only get 10 Rubles a day the same as the lazy lout who does next to nothing? This is a widely held opinion that results in most everybody under performing. China discovered this and shut down their state-run factories that produced mostly junk and allowed enough capitalism to have factories run such that they achieved "to each according to their abilities and work ethic." No work, no abilities, no food.

Belarus is a pure communism holdout and they are a perfect example of how that system fails from the standpoint of providing the necessities of life to its citizenry. They are an extremely poor nation, their productivity is terrible and their people have nothing compared to bordering capitalistic countries like Poland. Communism violates the pain and pleasure motivation that drives most people. We learn things and work to achieve pleasures (wealth, possessions) and we avoid things that bring pain (no wealth, no possession). People cannot get rich with communism. No matter how hard you work, you will only get the same as somebody who does not want to work.

Another fundamental flaw of communism is that somebody has to parcel out the "common" wealth. So a leadership hierarchy develops and surprise – the leaders get a little more than the non-leaders. Corruption on the part of the leadership is endemic to communism. Chairman Mao certainly has more pleasures and possessions than a rice paddy worker.

Of course, another fundamental flaw in communism is no say in what happens in your society and your life. The state decides where you will live, what you will do for a job, and of course, how much money you will make. Most humans like to decide on some of these things on their own. Thus, in 2010, communism has failed for most who have tried this form of government.

Dictatorship

Most communist societies are also dictatorships. A dictatorship is a country controlled by a single person not elected by citizenry and not controlled in any way by citizenry. The dictator imposes his or her mandates on the citizenry, usually with enforcement by police or military that is also under the dictator's control. Saddam Hussein was the dictator of Iraq. Fidel Castro is the dictator of Cuba. Dictators have the absolute powers of the old-time monarch. However, they were not given this absolute power by birth circumstance. Dictators often seized the power over a country's citizenry by police or military action. Dictators need the support of police or military to stay in power. The Cuban people have tried to revolt and obtain some say in their lives, but Castro's strong military quickly quenched any revolts, including the US backed Bay of Pigs invasion in the 1980's. Cuba is the poster child for communism as well as the poster child for dictatorship. It is possible to have communism with elected leaders. The monks and nuns in communal monasteries elect their leader. The "citizens" have a say in their leadership. This is not so with a dictatorship. Dictatorships can have capitalism. Spain was a capitalistic country ruled by a dictator (General Franco) until the late 1980's. People can own property and run a business but have no say in the public sector. This is run by the dictator.

The advantage of a dictatorship is the same as that of a monarchy: it is easier to accomplish public sector projects. A dictator does not have to get permission from a legislature or from the citizenry to do something. He or she just orders it and it happens. The disadvantage of a dictatorship is that it can be an unpleasant place to live if the dictates are bad or is you try to disagree with the dictator's dictates. Often, they are not amused by dissention.

Anarchy

How about "no government?" Some accounts of Native Americans suggest that some tribes or groups of Native Americans lived in a "society" with no government, no laws, and no leaders. There were families, but if a more powerful man wanted a person's wife, he could take her. Similarly, a person could kill another person with no "penalty" if that murder did not "bother" others in the group. Needless to say, such a system is not a society. It is below animal level in social order. Most animals living in a group have a leader and a methodology for achieving leadership (fighting) and the leader enforces order in the social group.

Anarchy was present in 2010 as the government in some African countries like Somalia. Civil wars destroyed the legitimate governments and various "gangs" with weapons control the citizenry. They can do anything that they want to the people since they have power to kill to improve their control over others. Afghanistan is the most egregious example of country ruled by anarchy. War lords with guns control citizens in separate regions and there are no activities for the common good like public schools and no country-wide facilities like roads or power generation. The citizens are completely at the mercy of the people with the guns.

No person in his or her right mind would want anarchy as their form of government, but they exist because the citizens do not have the weapons and leadership to fight the war lord system. This was the prevailing "form of government" in Japan for centuries, but at some time they had a unifying "Emperor" as head of the society, but the war lords with the guns controlled the people. They imposed their wishes on the people.

Many slum areas in larger cities throughout the world have anarchy as their form of government. The city of Kingston in Jamaica is "ruled" by a drug lord – there is no legitimate government. Cities in Mexico, Columbia, and many other places have no government in slum areas. These societies are controlled by the people with the guns and power.

Disasters like America's hurricane Katrina can turn societies into anarchies. Millions of American watched this happen in New Orleans. There was a complete and absolute breakdown of civility. People were behaving like animals, looting and robbing allegedly for self-preservation. So for those who think that any government is too much, you may not have a very pleasant life with no government.

Author's Commentary:

Our descriptions of forms of government that compete with our democracy may be a bit biased. I just returned from a trip to Brazil where I witnessed "no government" in a huge slum in Rio de Janeiro. A slum with maybe a million inhabitants was ruled by drug dealers and for the first time in decades, police entered the area to clean things up for a future hosting of World Cup Soccer. Scores of people were killed, buses were burned, cars were stopped on highways through the slums; their occupants were robbed and their vehicles burned. That was an example of anarchy – no government by conscious neglect on the part of the "legitimate" government. No government is not a good option.

Hopefully, we have made the case against communism and dictatorships so that leaves monarchy and a parliamentary form of democracy. There are some factors in America that feel that we should have a king or queen to take the public relations load off the shoulders of the President. Presidents currently spend more than 50% of their available time in a day doing non-leading things: smoozing. He or she must greet visiting dignitaries, go to state dinners, greet high schoolers on class tours to DC, fund raising, etc. There is little time left to run the country. A king or queen could help by taking care of these aspects of running a country. However, it is likely that Americans will not resurrect the royalty concept; it may only happen in certain sports.

Would a parliamentary democracy have an advantage over our present system? Our nearest neighbor, Canada has this system, but in 2010, they seem to have more acrimony in their system than ours. There seems to be more name calling between parties. On the other hand, America must do something to limit campaign costs – like the ten thousand pound limit in England. Our elected officials are so beholding to campaign contributions that they almost never legislate in the interests of the people – only the interests of significant contributors. This defeats the purpose of a democracy and must be stopped if our democracy is to survive another decade.

Questions

1.   How does a parliamentary monarchy function?
2.   If America were a monarchy who would be king?
3.   What is socialism?
4.   What is communism?
5.   Name five communist countries that existed in 2010.
6.   What is a dictatorship?
7.   Name five dictatorships that existed in 2010.
8.   What is anarchy?
9.   Cite a country where anarchy existed in 2010.
10.   what is "parliament"?

Related Reading

1.   Moore, Barrington, <u>Social Origins of Dictatorship and Democracy: Lord and Peasant in the Making of the Modern World</u>, 1993.

2.   Ghandi, Jennifer, <u>Political Institutions Under Dictatorship</u>, 2010.

3.   Pipes, Richard, <u>Communism: A History</u>, 2003.

4.   Douzinas, Costos and Fizek, Slovoj, <u>The Idea of Communism</u>, 2010.

5.   Warwick, Paul, <u>Government Survival in Parliamentary Democracies</u>, 2007.

6.   Barclay, Harold, and Comfort, Alex, <u>People Without Government: An Anthropology of Anarchy</u>, 1996.

Chapter 4

Our Political Parties

When America (the United States of America) was being created by the writing of our Constitution, there existed groups with different persuasions. Some wanted significant government control of "operations;" some wanted less. Some of our country founders were "city folk;" some were farmers and people who lived off the land. Needless to say, disparate groups were formed to lobby for each of their interests. Some of America's founders wanted a monarchy. They wanted to make George Washington King of America. Whatever the task faced by a group, it is natural to have the group morph into subgroups with differing opinions on how to perform the task at hand. This happens because we are all different in what makes us do what we do. Every person has a different data base in his or her brain, a different operating system, a different storage capability and different programming. Thus, there will always be disparate groups that evolve on any and all issues.

How Political Parties Function

Our Constitution does not spell out how candidates for office are created. The Constitution established requirements for candidates for some federal offices (President, Vice-president, Representative, Senator, etc.) but, does not establish a system for selecting candidates to run for most elected offices. The factions that existed at the foundation of America evolved into "political parties." They are essentially "like minded" individuals who agree to unify into a group that votes to achieve a government that is favorable to and in keeping with their ideologies. A later chapter addresses the differences between America's major political parties, but this chapter addresses how a political party committee functions: their legal status, their purpose, their objectives, their bylaws, their composition, their methodology, and the role that they play in America's democracy.

The Legal Status of Political Parties

America is ruled by laws. We have laws regarding your birth (need a certificate signed by somebody) and laws (many more) pertaining to your death (need a death certificate, will, heirs, executor, burial according to laws, can only be buried in certain places [not your garden], etc.). Political parties are covered by election laws and we have these laws at every level: federal, state, local. There are execution, eligibility and voting differences at every level, but political parties are "allowed" at every level and there are election laws to determine if a party and its candidates are allowed a place on the ballot for an elected office. For example, to get your name on a ballot for mayor of Nowhere, Arizona, you need to get 5% of the eligible voters in Nowhere to sign petitions saying that they may vote for you for mayor. There are only eight eligible voters in Nowhere so you only need to get 0.4 voters or one voter to sign a petition to get your name on the ballot. It gets tougher to meet petition requirements as the size of the voting entity grows. Five percent of Phoenix would be a significant number of signatures. Political parties solve that problem. They have "committee members" who are allowed by our election law to help a candidate gather enough signatures to earn a place on a ballot for office.

This concept has morphed into something more complex in our two major political parties. These parties have made additional "laws" that candidates must conform to in order to be eligible to be their candidate. For example, some have screening committees composed of whomever their bylaws say, who can determine which candidate gets endorsed as the party candidate where there are a number of party members who want the elected office. The presidential conventions run by the Democrats and Republicans are the ultimate example of candidate screening committees. There are representatives from every state and they have to agree as a block who to support at each ballot and the states compete in different votes, and lobbying is used to sway states. And so the process goes in order to arrive at one candidate for president and one for vice-president.

Primaries are used at the state level to select candidates and each candidate at the primary level must garner enough committee supporters to meet petition requirements. Primaries can be used at every government level for every elected office and the results of primary elections trumps the wishes of any party screening committee or within-party votes. Primaries allow members of a political party to vote on who they want to be their candidate on a ballot for elected office. Most voting entities require registration in a particular party to vote for a party candidate, but some states, etc., allow others to also vote in primaries.

So the legal status of political parties is that they supply candidates for elected office according to laws covering how primaries are conducted and who is eligible to sign petitions and to carry petitions, but there are no laws on forming a political party or how they function. For example, in the 2010 race for governor of New York, there were candidates from political parties formed specifically for this particular election for governor. The "Rent's Too Damn High Party" was formed to allow one person to run for the single position of Governor of New York. Somehow, this new party managed to fulfill the petition requirement in the time allowed by the election law. However, the "party" may be dissolved after the election (he did not win). Political parties can be as simple as a single person with followers or as complex as the Democrat and Republican Parties with committees at every government level, in every state, in every city, in every town, in every county in the US.

Purpose of Political Parties

The purpose of a political party is to unit like-minded individuals so that they can promote their ideology through the election of people who share their ideology to public office.

Needless to say, the ideologies of America's political parties have changed significantly over the past 200 years, but there have always been opposing ideologies. At the start, there were the farmers and the non-farmers. Around the turn of the century, there were opposing views on how to deal with a resurgence of British influence. Mid-century, the big issue was slavery and political parties took opposing sides.

Political parties allow a voice to be reckoned with. A simple citizen is almost always ignored by elected officials at every level. Only significant members gather attention. If you believe in a sustainable society for example, you can communicate with every senator or congressman or woman and you will likely receive zero replies (I've tried it). All politicians who want to stay in the business need large numbers of voters supporting them. They cannot afford to spend time on "one vote." They will deal with organizations with significant membership, but not individuals. Political parties solve this problem. If you become active in a political party, you can lobby for sustainable-society candidates or even try to make a sustainable society (or whatever) part of the party's election platform. Thus, political parties allow America's citizens a way to unite with other like minded citizens to promote their causes by promoting election of citizens with their ideology to office.

Objective of Political Parties

Every action has both a purpose and an objective. The purpose of this book is to inform and educate on how America's democracy works, the details, the philosophies. The objective is to improve and continue our democracy. Our democracy is threatened on many fronts. The objective of most political parties is similar. Their objective is to continue the America envisioned in our Constitution. Some political parties like the "Communist Party" have an objective of communal or state ownership of property. This objective is not commensurate with America's Constitution. Thus, we cannot say that all political parties have survival of America as we know it as an objective. However, all of the major political parties have objectives of an

America based upon our Constitution. These parties differ in their approach to this objective. For example, the Libertarian Party wants America to run with a minimum of government interference into our personal lives. On the other extreme is the Democratic Party which promotes government control of Americans from cradle to grave. The Conservative and Republican Parties are someplace in between these two extremes in "management philosophy." In summary, most political parties have continuation of a functioning Constitutional democracy as their overall objective.

Anatomy of a Political Party

As mentioned previously, political parties have the legal status of a social club – like a school PTA, group of marathon runners, etc. Their makeup and operation can be anything. The committee that I belong to calls itself the "City of yyyy, xxxx Committee. They have a set of "rules" that is supposed to determine how they operate. Their stated objective is

- To ensure good government
- To provide resources and support to elect xxxx's to public office
- To prepare and encourage the most qualified xxxx's to be candidates for public office

The committee has a chairperson, vice-chairperson, secretary, treasurer, and a county representative. There are "leaders" elected to head campaign efforts in the various election districts of the town. The election districts are legal election boundaries established by the party in power after the once-in-a-decade federal census. Election districts are important because they define a geographic voter block that may have their own representative to a legislature. There are also ward leaders who "lead" geographic divisions of the town or city and each ward may have a representative to a legislature. So committee members need to select internal leaders for ward, election district, and county levels. Of course, at the town or city level, the legislative requirements vary with every city, town and county in the country, but the party committees address them. The leaders of a party form an executive committee. The workers in a political party are called "committee members" and they are "elected" in a way. Their names are listed on the designating petitions that they circulate prior to every election. The qualifications for a committee member are:

1. Must be an enrolled xxxx voter
2. Must reside in "Town or City of yyyy"
3. Must carry petitions that include their name
4. Must actively support the activities of the "Town or City of yyyy" committee

The district and ward leaders must reside in their respective ward and districts and the officers shall reside in the municipality (town or city). The Committee rules spell out the specific duties of each officer, how they are to be elected, and what happens when there is a vacancy.

Meetings/Elections

The committee rules dictate regular monthly meetings. The meetings can be attended by the public, but the committee does not publicize the meetings. Thus, non-committee members usually are invited by committee members. Committee members vote on all committee positions using a secret ballot and the winner is simply the person with the most votes. Only committee members can vote in election of officers or on designation of candidates. Town or city committee members can also be committee members of the county xxxx committee. As such, they vote on county committee officers and candidates at the county and state level. An executive (town leader) from every town and city in a county sits on the county executive committee. This committee designates members from this executive committee to attend meetings and vote at the state party level for candidates for governor and president. So there is a large hierarchy in the committees of the national political parties. In fact, we are still not done. There is a national xxxx committee usually in DC, which runs the presidential candidate convention. They also control discretionary funding to candidates throughout the nation.

Their Role

Political parties supply candidates for public office. We have election laws that only allow us to vote for candidates who earn a position on the ballot and it usually requires the people resources of political parties to meet petition requirements. Very wealthy people hire a staff to garner petitions. They can bypass political parties or start their own like Ross Perot did to run for president in the 1990's. Theoretically, a person can be a write-in candidate for any office, but this is a difficult path to office if the intended office is a state or federal one. However, in 2010 a US senator was elected by write-in. So it can happen.

The road to elected office is much easier through political parties and if one opts for one of the two major parties, the machinery is in place to help candidates get elected at every level. Political parties also train Americans on how to run for elected office. Running an election campaign is not an easy task. Where does one start? Participation in a political party committee provides an "apprenticeship" in politics and campaigning. Political parties are the brunt of many complaints about our democracy, but because they supply our leaders, they need participation (and improvement) by all Americans. They allow Americans to really participate in their democracy.

Strengths of Political Parties

A participative government cannot exist without a mechanism to allow citizens to participate. In a true democracy, all citizens have the opportunity for leadership positions and all citizens can input (vote, etc.) on who the leaders should be. Although political parties are not addressed in the Constitution, we have a two party system that fulfills this necessary part of a democracy. They take care of the details of how citizens can participate in their government, their destiny.

Our system allows for as many political parties that meet the petition requirements of the election laws. We can have parties that promote drugs and prostitution, parties that propose polygamy, parties that oppose high rents, etc. A significant strength of our political party system is that all "groups" can organize and promote candidates of office that support their specific platform.

Because our Constitution does not limit political parties or how they operate, these "parties" are open to all citizens. However, young people (under 18 years old) are not allowed to vote. One of the ways that they can participate in their government is through "Young Libertarians" or other "subcommittees" of the main political parties that may have a permanent ballot position. Some political parties have "auxiliaries" for spouses of committee members. These party "subcommittees" serve to allow citizens not allowed to vote a chance to participate in their democracy. Many colleges and universities have "political parties" on campus to promote their causes even though they may not propose candidates because they may not be able to meet residency requirements to vote in local elections. Anybody in America who is interested in a career in public service can find a party to their liking and participate in their activities at any age. A 10-year-old can make get out the vote phone calls and all parties welcome this help. Political parties can be a vehicle for universal participation in the governmental process.

Weaknesses of America's Political Parties

I hope that we have conveyed the message that political parties have evolved into an integral part of America's democracy. A democracy needs a facility for training people to be our leaders. Leadership in a democracy requires dealing with diverse opinions, diverse interests, and diverse cultures. Political parties train people to do this. Public office requires that a person have effective communication skills. Political parties offer great opportunities for public speaking and written communication (and electronic communication). A democracy needs leaders who know how our system works – the organization chart for America. Political parties supply this information. Running for office at various levels lets people learn the system. It also allows people to live with our Constitution and learn its vagaries. Political parties are a good thing. So why do so may Americans look at them with distrust? Why do the majority of Americans feel that all politicians are corrupt, crooks?

The short answer is: many are. The general public only gets to see the corruption in politics when somebody gets caught violating a law. The free press is our only vehicle to ferret out corruption in government and in 2011, all Americans know that the free press is in failure mode. They are losing their foundation, advertising revenue, to electronic media. Can electronic media take its place? No! In 2011, there is no independent source of unbiased information on government functions or elected leaders. America is on the brink of losing review of our government for honesty, accountability, and ethics with the demise of the free press.

Adult Americans seem to be too busy with their careers (and soccer, etc.) to get involved in participating in their democracy. Old Americans usually vote, but their participation usually stops there because they are too busy doing old-people stuff. So who's in political parties? Who is running them? In my case, the committee that I belong to, the answer is public employees. The members of the executive committee of my party all hold elected offices. The committee consists of about 95% public employees. In fact, most work for the city party leader. The net result is a local government of, by and for the public sector, but paid for by the private sector. Corruption is complete and absolute.

Author's Commentary

Unless Americans at every age level start to participate in their democracy by active participation in political parties or government at some level, America will not survive. The present incestuous system will fail. If we do not have participation on the part of farmers, pharmacists, roofers, electricians, carpenters, and cleaning people, we will have a government composed entirely of politicians who have never held a job outside of the public sector. Our last three presidents never held any job, but public sector ones. They have no idea what America is like on the factory floor. And that is probably why we are in the fix we are in.

Soccer moms and dads go to great lengths and personal sacrifice to get their kids active in sports and attend their games. How much effort do they expend in exposing their children to our democracy and how it works? We do not teach our children how to run the country that they will be called upon to serve and lead. Young adults are too busy with school or looking for work to get involved in politics. If politics was working properly, they would not be looking for a job. They would have one.

Questions

1. What is a political committee?
2. Describe the hierarchy/structure of political committees.
3. How are candidates for elected office chosen?
4. Who oversees the operation of political committees in America?
5. What is an election district and how are they established?
6. Who funds political parties?
7. What criterion must be established for a political party to get their candidate on a ballot?
8. Who is eligible to become a member of a political committee?
9. What is the origin of political parties?
10. What is the legal status of political parties?

Related Reading

1. Adkins, Randall E., <u>The Evolution of Political Parties, Campaigns, and Elections: Landmark documents1878 – 2007</u>, 2008

2. Hershey, Margaret, <u>Political Parties in America</u>, 14th Ed, 2010

3. Ware, Alan, <u>Political Parties and Party Systems</u>, 1995

4. Diamond, Larry and Gunther, Richard, <u>Political Parties and Democracy</u>, 2001

5. Sabato, Larry and Ernst, Howard R., <u>Encyclopedia of American Political Parties and Elections,</u> 2007

Chapter 5

Our Government Appointees

I do not know if other "democracies" let their elected leader appoint the people who control the functioning of government, but here in America, we do. The US Constitution allows the president to establish "helpers" to assist him or her in running the country. There are fifteen "cabinet" level helpers. People are appointed to run the military; the defense department; to negotiate with other countries; to the state department; to manage the tax revenues; to the treasury department; to enforce laws; the attorney general department and so on. These are called "cabinet" positions for a reason dating back to Andrew Jackson's administration. He allegedly had his advisors come secretly into the White House by the kitchen door. His advisers were called "kitchen cabinet advisors" and the "cabinet" term is still used for official advisors. Cabinet members now have the title of Secretary of xxx. What citizens need to know is that the cabinet heads meet frequently with the president and essentially, run the government for him. Each department head has a staff and a budget and areas of responsibility. The four cabinet positions that we just mentioned (treasury, military, state, attorney general) have been established for most of the life of America's democracy. New cabinet positions have been created, combined, or deleted at the pleasure of presidents over the decades. President George W. Bush created the Homeland Security position during his administration to deal with a new type of threat to the country – terrorism attacks by crazed individuals and groups – not armies. Other cabinet positions evolved similarly to meet specific needs. Cabinet members are appointed by the president and confirmed by Congress at the start of an administration. They serve at the pleasure of the president and vacancies are filled by the president (with congressional approval).

Department of State

There is an obvious need in any government to have a function to maintain surveillance on other countries and negotiate with them in the country's interest. The Department of State maintains embassies in most nations of the world with a staff headed by an ambassador. Ambassadors are appointed by the president and usually serve for the term of the president, but can be replaced by the president. Recalling an ambassador from a country is currently used as a sign of America's displeasure with happenings in a particular country. Embassies offer aid to American citizens having problems in a particular country and often they have public relation functions to improve America's image in a particular country. The USA allows embassies from other countries with which we have ambassadorial relations. They usually have their embassy in DC and often maintain "sub-embassies" called consulates in big cities, like New York. Consulates usually supply visas to US citizens when a particular country requires a US citizen to have one to travel in that country. This is probably the only way that ordinary citizens have the opportunity to deal with the Department of State. The head of the Department of State is the first cabinet member in line for the presidency in the event that something happened to the president, vice president, and speaker of the house.

Department of Defense

Like the Department of State, the need for a country to have such a function is obvious. There probably has never been "peace on earth" since original sin. Some groups are always warring someplace on our planet. America's Department of Defense has traditionally been chaired by a non-military person and all of our military units -- Army, Navy, Marines, and Air Force – report to the Secretary of Defense. The Constitution does not require that the Secretary of the Department of Defense be a civilian, but this tradition started after World War II, and has prevailed since that time. This is probably a good idea since many countries have had the head of their military become so strong that he or she takes over the country by force and the head of the military becomes the head of state. These people have the guns, so who can argue with them. A civilian leader can fire a general or admiral who may get too power hungry and coup-prone.

Department of the Treasury

This department was one of the first ones established when the democracy was formed. It is the keeper of the funds that the government needs to function. This department is responsible for the Federal Reserve System that holds the country's wealth in gold. They have every citizen's friend – the Internal Revenue Service – to collect taxes. They also have the staff and power to control the banking system. They control interest rates between banks which distill down to a determining factor for interest rates that we, the people, are given by banks. The Department of the Treasury prints the paper money that we use and mints the coins that eventually end up in America's slot machines. The treasury also taxes corporations, cigarettes, alcohol, gasoline, and anything else that Congress will allow.

The Department of Justice

The Department of Justice is comprised of the Attorney General's office and the Federal Bureau of Investigation (FBI). The correct title for the Attorney General is Secretary of the Department of Justice. However in 2009, it was known to citizens as the attorney general function. The attorney general, like all cabinet positions, is appointed by the sitting president with Congressional approval and he or she serves at the pleasure of the president. The Attorney General is responsible for enforcement of federal laws.

The FBI is the well-known American police organization that gets involved in interstate crimes. They are part of the Department of Justice. The Department of Justice is also supposed to prevent monopolies in business and industry and they are responsible for representing the United States in cases brought before the Supreme Court. They are our (we citizens) lawyers. The Solicitor General is a presidential appointee working in the Department of Justice and he or she argues for the US in cases before the Supreme Court.

Department of Agriculture

This department was started after the Civil War to help farmers by providing them with weather information and other assistance to help rebuild the farm economy. America had an agrarian society at the time with about 90% of the population making their living on the farm. Since World War II, this department has been headed mostly by politicians from "farm" states or prominent farmers. This department oversees the USDA which inspects food processing facilities and shares responsibility for ensuring the safety of America's food supply. They have many programs to help farmers in times of draught or other disasters. They are responsible for the Food Stamp Program that aids many needy US families.

Department of Education

This department has only been in existence since 1980, and their charge is to "oversee" educational systems in the US. Every state has an education department and leader with the same responsibility; every school in America belongs to the district or group that usually coincides with a taxation boundary. A city school district will tax all city residents for their schools; a town will have a school district that taxes town residents for their schools. Each district has a head, a superintendent or the like that makes educational decisions for the district. Each district will likely have an elected board that approves or not plans of the district leader. An expectation of the Department of Education is that they do what they can to ensure that every American child gets a proper education and that the quality of that education is the same in remote rural areas as in wealthy big city suburbs.

Department of Housing and Urban Development

This is another product of post World War II America (1965). It was created by Congress to help provide shelter to all Americans. What this department did in the 1960's and 1970's is build large low-income tenements in all cities. They were intended to improve the living arrangements of poor people who had been living in run-down 50 to 75 year old city homes. What happened is that they destroyed many well-built single family homes to make room for the towering tenements, and thus, played havoc with most downtowns in America. Then the tenements became centers for every sort of crime and places where the bad kids teach all other kids to be bad.

Thus, this department has poured untold billions into America's city centers and the net effect is most American cities are decreasing in size in deference to suburbs and have failing schools. Our cities are our epicenters of poverty and crime.

Department of Commerce

This American government function is supposed to promote business, jobs, and wealth in America. They supervise the Census Bureau, US Weather Service, the US Patent and Trademark function, the Library of Congress, copyrights, and economic forecasts and results. They help businesses in America sell their goods in other countries through liaison with embassies and consulates throughout the world. This function is redundant in every state and every municipality. Almost all municipalities in America have a Chamber of Commerce. These groups are not government funded and they self-fund programs to promote business in their municipality. The functioning of the Department of Commerce could probably benefit from a formal relationship with local chambers of commerce.

Department of Health and Human Services

This is also a post World War II creation of ever increasing government. The functions of this department that are of most concern to average citizens are the Food and Drug Administration (FDA) and the Center for Disease Control

(CDC). The FDA determines if a particular drug or medical device can be used in the USA, and the Center for Disease Control monitors the health of people using statistics and determines how healthy America's citizens are. There are hundreds of health-related programs sponsored by this department and an important function is the administration of Medicare, the health insurance program that most people over 65 years of age in America rely on for health services. This department also makes grants to universities to promote medical research. This function has become vital to America's democracy, but they need to do more, especially in the area of bringing new drugs and treatments from other countries to America.

Department of Labor

This department was about 100 years old in 2009, and it was created to address issues with workers in America's burgeoning manufacturing industry. The Department of Labor established the rules that we Americans work by: what constitutes a work day; a work week, how many days can we work without a day off, guidelines on overtime pay, etc. For the most part, this department has made a contribution to the American citizenry. When the industrial revolution hit America, children under 10 were working 12-hour days in coal mines. Children now can be children, at least until 14 years of age, and they cannot work in factories until they are 18. I started working at seven, but only easy jobs like delivering newspapers and selling ice cream to factory workers. Now we Americans could use some Department of Labor help in banning work after 70. I am getting awfully tired.

Department of Transportation

The Department of Transportation has oversight of America's interstate highway system. Funding for US highways funnels through this department and from that standpoint, they are an important part of every American's life. We are a mobile society. We, essentially, live in our automobiles. This department controls every airport, train, metro, shipping, and harbors. They fund the National Transportation Safety Board which investigates all plane, train, and ship accidents to make regulations to prevent recurrence. The air traffic controllers in all US airports work for this agency.

Department of Homeland Security

This department was created by President George W. Bush after the 2001 attack on America by Muslim terrorists. This department combined existing American protection agencies like the border patrol, customs, and emergency preparedness into one organization with more that 150,000 employees. They established many new border patrol offices and initiated many steps to inspect people, vehicles, and materials coming into the country in order to identify any potentially dangerous person, vehicle, or materials attempting to enter the country. The Transportation Safety Administration (TSA) inspects all airline passengers and luggage on every domestic flight leaving all US airports.

The newly combined emergency preparedness arm of Homeland Security displayed consummate ineptitude when a 2005 hurricane inundated the City of New Orleans. The city has never recovered and probably never will. This department was formed in a crisis and it appears that its formation was not thought out and it functions like a massive "Keystone Cops" organization. It needs to be redesigned into something more manageable and based upon common sense. America's government response to disasters and threats appears to just spend money on these things and not demand results from the spent money – an opinion.

Department of Veteran Affairs

America takes good care of the men and women who have fought for the country in wars. This was not always a cabinet position, because the federal government opted to provide pensions and medical treatments to veterans of the Civil

War. What is now the Building Museum in Washington was a massive building built to house an organization to help Civil War veterans. The function became a cabinet position in 2002. This department oversees many veterans' hospitals around the country that provide medical treatments free of charge to veterans. This department also oversees benefits to wounded veterans, burials, and family benefits for military killed in action.

Department of Energy

This department was established in 1971 with the charge of ensuring the energy supply of America and the safe use of nuclear energy. They mostly function as a source of funding for energy – related research and development. For example, if you wanted funding to develop a new type of solar collector to convert solar energy to electrical energy, you would apply to the Department of Energy (DOE). The Department of Energy continually funds activities such as nuclear fusion which have the potential of being important new sources of energy.

Other Significant Government Departments

A newly elected president also appoints heads to:

1. Office of Management and Budget which helps to president prepare the federal budget and has oversight on federal funding and spending.

2. Environmental Protection Agency which has responsibility at the federal level for policies relating to pollution and land use. They control our green house gas commitment to the world.

3. Director of Drug Control which has the charge of reducing the use of illegal drugs and crimes related to this activity.

4.   US Trade Representative which has responsibility for America's trade policies with other countries.

5.   The Vice President, who has responsibility for breaking ties in the Senate, is advisor to the president, and special advocate for the president.

6.   White House Chief of Staff which has responsibility for the president's time. This person directs the president's daily activities, who he or she sees, who he or she meets with.

7. US Postal Service which has responsibility for our post office and mail delivery system. This position is not under a cabinet head, but rather under the Executive Branch. The Postmaster General, the head of this
organization, is appointed by the president.

8. Central Intelligence Agency was created in 1947 to provide the president (and Congress) with information appointed by the president and approved by Congress. They are America's "spy" agency.

9.   Social Security Administration is America's welfare system for people over 65 and for people under 65 with disabilities. It is the most costly program of the US government – 37% of the government's expenditures in 2009 and some 60 million Americans were receiving benefits in 2010.

All of these positions have cabinet level status. They are part of the president's management team. They work directly for the president at his or her pleasure. They are appointed by the president and are charged with assisting the president in certain areas.

Strengths of Our Government Agencies

America has an agency/department to deal with every aspect of running a country. You name it, we have it. America is particularly good at military response. We are good to our veterans. Besides benefits, veterans of our wars receive preference in obtaining government jobs and promotions. The taxing system is very complex, but in general, US citizens pay less tax than most other nations with our degree of civilization. Over the last four or five decades, America has been the world leader in diplomacy (State Department) with other nations of the world. We have been giving money to support many fledgling democracies and we are the first to offer help to others in the time of natural disasters. America offers help to just about any country that asks for it.

The Health and Human Services Department provides a great service to America's citizens and peoples around the world by sponsoring medical research in our universities and research institutions. This is where our new medicines and pharmaceutical specials come from. Funding research at universities provides our population, our medical professionals, and our medical experts.

America's Department of Labor has provided us with a plethora of laws to preclude the need for unions to obtain safe and equitable working conditions for all Americans who work. Our Department of Transportation has given the United States an incredible system of interstate highways. There is probably none better in the world. We can do just about any place in the continental United States in a four-lane divided highway with speed limits in excess of 65 mph – quite a feat.

Finally, America's Social Security System may be the most generous in the world. The United States gives all retired Americans enough money to find reasonable shelter, food, and medical care. We also give these benefits to all who claim to be unable to work for medical reasons. Again, no other nation is so magnanimous to its citizenry.

Weakness of Our Government Agencies

The president of the US gets to control almost every aspect of the lives of US citizens through his appointments of leadership in these many organizations which touch every aspect of the lives of Americans. The tax people from the Department of Treasury (IRS) determine our tax burden, the Department of Defense determines the draft and who gets called to fight wars, the Environmental Protection Agency dictates the mileage we get on cars, the FDA determines what drugs we can take and what operations are approved; the Transportation Security Administration (TSA) which is part of Homeland Security, pats us down in airports; the Postal Service delivers our mail (when they get a chance); the USDA (Agriculture Department) determines if the meat that we eat is safe; the Department of Transportation's Federal Aviation Agency (FAA) controls our airplanes; the Department of Transportation controls our interstate highways; the Department of Labor determines our workplace rules; the Social Security Administration controls our retirement funding, and so on down the list. The president of the United States has great power over out personal lives by agencies which citizens have no control over or even input into.

A fundamental deficiency of government agencies charged with "needed" responsibilities is that there is no accountability to the citizens who pay for there functions. We saw the complete and absolute failure of the US federal government in dealing with the hurricane Katrina disaster. However, none of the responsible persons lost their jobs. Nothing was done to reassure citizens that another similar failure would occur in a future disaster.

In 2010, we are seeing exponential growth in TSA activity in airports. In some airports it seems like there are more TSA agents than passengers. Do Americans want this level of "security?" Does it work? The TSA's own audits have shown that it really does not work. Test explosives continue to get through.

Author's Commentary

American citizens deserve accountability from government agencies. An annual review of benefits vs costs might identify government functions that are not delivering the citizen benefits that they are supposed to deliver. Budgets should be zero-based and budgeting for the year should be based upon delivery of needed benefits to citizens.

Another fundamental flaw in our democracy is that every leadership position in government agencies at every level of government are patronage jobs. This practice compromises the functions. Why should a person persevere and be innovative and hard working and do a good job in the Agriculture Department when the leadership job will be given to a woman from New York City who was a successful fund raiser for the President in that area. A better way may be to have consultants to the presidents in each area rather than patronage managers – there could be a labor consultant, agriculture consultant, transportation consultant, etc. This would keep needed organizations intact through president changes and allow persons in these organizations to achieve leadership positions based upon performance of the department's task, not fund raising.

These government agencies control the details of the lives of all Americans and citizens deserve better performance, some measure of accountability, and qualified leaders.

Questions

1.   What is the President's "cabinet"?
2.   Name the cabinet positions.
3.   What are the responsibilities of the State Department?

4.   What are the responsibilities of the Defense Department?
5.   What are the functions of the Department of Justice?
6.   What is the mission of the Department of Housing and Urban Development?
7.   What are the responsibilities of the Commerce Department?
8.   What are the functions of the Department of Labor, the Transportation Department, Homeland Security, Veterans Affairs, and the Department of Energy?
9.   What government entity runs the Post Office, the CIA, the EPA, and the Social Security Administration?
10.   What government agency do ambassadors report to?
11.   What government agency controls FEMA?
12.   What is a czar and how many czars existed in America's government in 2010?
13.   What government agency has oversight of national parks? National forests? Oil rights?
14.   What agency does OSHA fall under?
15.   What agency approves what medical devices can be used in the US?
16.   What agency does the IRS report to?
17.   What agency does the Coast Guard fall under?
18.   What agency do airport security agents fall under?
19.   What agency do airport controllers fall under?
20.   What agency does the FBI fall under?

Related Reading

1.   Justice, Keith L, <u>Presidents, Vice Presidents, Cabinet Members, Supreme Court Justices 1789-2003, Vital and Official Data,</u>   2010

2.   Mol, Ronald C., <u>The President's Cabinet: Evolution, Alternatives, and Proposals for change</u>, 2004.

3.   Parker, Nancy Winslow, <u>The President's Cabinet and how it Grew,</u> 1992.

4.   Hinsdale, Mary Louise, <u>A History of the President's Cabinet (Volume 1)</u>, 2010.

5.   Adams, George Burton, <u>Federal Government: Its Functions and Methods</u>, 2010.

Chapter 6

Our State and Local Governments

State Organizations

When America was formed there were 13 states headed by governors who were appointed by the King of England. The states agreed to fight the revolution; the states agreed to form a union with a constitution. So states were important at the start of the United States. Eventually, the states that made up early America developed constitutions that formed state organizations that mimicked the federal government. There are now nuances in minor areas, but in 2009, all states in the US are headed by a governor; they all have legislatures; they all have a police function; they all have a comptroller/treasurer; they all have a vice governor (generally known as "lieutenant" governor. They all have a clerk or secretary. They all have courts – a justice system. Some governors run with their lieutenant governor, like the president runs with a vice president. Some run separately. Thus, all states have an executive branch, a legislative branch, and a judicial branch.

Not all states elect all of the heads of departments. Some department heads are appointed. In New York State, for example, the governor and lieutenant governor run as a team and comptroller, attorney general, and judges run separately. Some states have a secretary of state to keep records. The comptroller collects taxes and controls the states coffers. The attorney general represents the state in the courts. The lieutenant governor often plays only a minor role in the executive branch of state government. However, in 2008 to 2009, two governors were removed from office (one was impeached, the other resigned before he was impeached) and the lieutenant governors became governors. Thus, they really do have an important role.

All states have a plethora of agencies that report to the various branches; New York has more than 10,000. The state

65

legislatures are often patterned after congress. There is an upper and a lower house (bicameral) and they can be called different things. In New York, the upper house is called the senate and the lower house is called the assembly. Each state is divided into districts and each district has a representative to the upper house and to the lower house.

Congress has 435 members, one from each congressional district. A congressional district consists of 600,000 citizens and the geographic boundaries are established by the party in power when redistricting occurs. Redistricting occurs after each census which is taken every 10 years. Tinkering with district boundaries to achieve political goals (like mostly residents in your party) is called gerrymandering and it has become a way of life for Republicans and Democrats. My congressional district contains a section that is one street wide (shoreline on one of the Great Lakes) and 50 miles long. State legislative districts are approved by the state legislature, and some states have lots of people (like 400) in their legislature and some may only have 40. State legislatures must approve the state budget and thus, they control state spending for roads, police, education, parks, environmental, etc. All states have a military, often in the form of the National Guard. These are part-time military that can be called up by the governor to help in times of emergencies. In some states, the state legislature positions are part-time and the legislators hold other jobs.

Town Governments

Villages are the smallest unit of government in a state. They may be only a few people, but villages are combined with open land to form towns that may have a significant physical area. Villages can have a type of government, but in most states, towns are responsible for most services. For example, a village may have a mayor and a council to control village affairs, but highway maintenance and often, schools are maintained at a town level and the town may contain several villages. Town governments usually have an elected head and vice head, an elected board and maybe elected clerk, treasurer, public works

head, assessor and justice. Towns usually have a school district
or several to fund schools. These districts have the power to tax.
Special districts can be formed to pay for street lights, sewers,
and the like.

County Governments

All states are divided into counties and country
government is higher in hierarchy than town and village
governments. Counties administer state laws. There are more
than 3,000 counties in America and most have and elected head,
a manager, supervisor, etc, and some elected department heads,
like sheriff, clerk, district attorney, and judges. Counties have a
legislative branch that can be a one-house (unicameral) assembly
– county legislature with representatives from each town or some
smaller legislative body. The legislators are usually elected.

City Governments

Some Americans may be lucky enough to pay taxes to a
state, county, town, village, and city for the same residence.
Usually, state constitutions define what it takes to be a city –
sometimes at least 50,000 people. Sometimes it takes more.
Cities need a charter or constitution and they have powers not
available to towns and villages. Each state has rules as to what
constitutes a city. Cities have an elected head; they can have an
elected mayor or city manager hired by the city legislature. With
a mayor type of government, the mayor may appoint department
heads and he or she interfaces with the unicameral council for
approvals and funding. The legislators are elected. In the city
manager system, an elected city council (assembly, etc.) hires a
business manager to oversee the day-to-day operations and the
city manager hires and fires department heads. The city manager
serves at the pleasure of the city council. Some cities have
elected commissioners to run the city versus a leader who hires
and fires department heads. A city run by a committee probably

runs as smoothly as an automobile designed by a committee (a camel was a horse designed by a committee).

In summary, America's democracy contains enough "sub-governments" at several levels. They copy congress at almost every state level. The intent of having these levels of government is to allow citizens from different geographical areas leadership that addresses local concerns.

Strengths of America's State and Local Government

It is a natural tendency for people with like interests and backgrounds to band together. This is how towns and cities were established. The city where I live had two waterfalls on a significant river as the magnet for people to reside nearby. The waterfalls were harnessed to run mills. Mills needed workers' workers need services – a city was the result. It was a mill city to start and the people living there wanted roads to market their flour and other products produced by the mills and factories that used the hydro-power from the falls. Thus, there were local interests wanting better transportation, interstate roads.

Another city that I lived in had copper mining as their local interest. They shipped their copper by boat so they had local interests for good harbors on the Great Lakes. This scenario is duplicated wherever people in the US congregated and state, county, town, city, and village governments sprouted to address local concerns. Thus, America's Constitution allowed for local governments in the form of state promoted regional interests of its citizenry. The states in turn allowed county, town, city, and village governments to address concerns in various parts of a state. In New York State, the local interests in the New York City area are different from the interests in the Buffalo area of the state. A significant strength of our democracy is regional representation. We have elected representatives at several levels of government with responsibility to legislate to help citizens in their local area have what they need from government to live and prosper in their locale.

Another significant advantage of thousands of local governments is that we Americans can change our local government by moving. Americans are free to move anyplace that they want in the USA. This is not the case in many countries. If we find the property taxes in New York unmanageable, we can move to Florida where they are only 25% of the property taxes in New York. If we find business regulations in New York oppressive and business threatening, we can relocate the business to North Carolina where they partner with business rather than regarding new business as an entity to be controlled.

Many aspects of life are best governed and managed at the local level. For example, education, roads, police, environmental issues, infrastructure, mass transit, etc. America does this. We have all these levels of government to "personalize" our democracy to its citizens.

The Weaknesses of America's State and Local Governments

We have now covered the hierarchy of government in America: Federal, State, County, City, Town, and Village. Each level of government is supposed to supply services to constituents, but do they? Take the example of education. The only public employees that interface with students work for school districts, not the federal government, the state government, not the county government. Some cities control their school district, but another level of government, the school district, actually hires teachers, builds schools, and decides what to teach students. The federal and state governments all have education departments which supposedly set standards for education, but they are so removed from students that their standards could be irrelevant.

Most readers, at this point, probably are feeling that America has too much government. Too much is probably an understatement. It reminds me of the money changers that I encountered in China in 1983. Whenever we needed some Yuan, we informed our Chinese Government hosts and three people would show up with a suitcase of Yuan. We would make our request to exchange Dollars to Yuan to person number one. He or she would write our request on a slip of paper and hand it to person number two. Person number two approved or not the transaction and handed the paper to person number three who handed us our Yuan. Three persons did the work that is now done by an ATM machine. Many government jobs are simply make-work jobs that create all sorts of barriers to business, manufacturing, and commerce in general. Excessive government at every level is making it impossible to compete in a global economy. Government jobs are great gigs: lots of money, lots of holidays, great benefits, guaranteed for life. Unfortunately, American citizens who have to work two jobs to survive cannot afford to support three people who could be replaced by a machine (which does a better job).

Author's Commentary

America's government in 2011 is simply incommensurate with America's economy. The loss of manufacturing has eliminated the middle class. We now have the wealthy, government employees, and the poor, and a significant number of government leaders are in the wealthy class. America has more government than the $10.00 per hour jobs that are available to us can pay for. Government, at all levels, must be reduced to the point where no government at any level is funded in any way by borrowing. If a village has a tax on income from all sources of $100,000, then that, by law, is all that it can spend on government.

America has a job crisis in 2011: there are none. So laying off government workers to balance the budget would make unemployment worse. It does not have to be. Government *workers' salaries and benefits need to be reduced to market rate ($10.00/hour like us) and they can keep their jobs and we can have a balanced budget.*

All unnecessary activities need to be eliminated. For example, last season I kept my sailboat next to a New York State naval vessel. It never moved all season, but some State organization has an armed steel vessel that probably cost $500,000 and served no purpose that I know of. New York State got a new governor in 2009 and he admitted early on that he had no idea what most of the 10,000 state departments that reported to him did. America must trim government and only allow fully-funded functions with demonstrated common good to exist.

Questions

1. What elected officers are common to state government?
2. What is a county and what is its role in America's government?
3. What is the legal difference between a village, a town, and a city in America's local government system, and who establishes them?
4. What does a state comptroller do?
5. What does a state attorney general do?
6. What is the role of village government?
7. What is the role of town government?
8. What is the role of country government?
9. What is the role of city government?
10. What is gerrymandering?

Related Reading

1. Bowman, Ann O'M, and Kearney, Richard, <u>State and Local Government</u>, 2010.

2. Saffell, David and Basehart, Harry, <u>State and Local Government</u>, 2008.

3.   Magleby, David B., Light, Paul C. and Nemacheck,
        Christine L., State and Local Politics: Government by
        the People, 2011.

4.   Donovan, Todd, Mooney, Christopher Z. and Smith,
        Daniel, State and Local Politics: Institutions and
        Reform, 2010.

Chapter 7

Electing Judges

The Supreme Court was created by America's Constitution as the arm of government that ultimately decides if a piece of legislation from Congress or act of the executive branch is allowable under America's Constitution. The Constitution also stated that congress may from "time to time" establish "inferior" courts that they deem necessary. Boy have they deemed! We have judges in the Supreme Court, the Court of Appeals, and all the lesser courts on down to the local courts – the state supreme court, city courts, town justices, and assorted other local courts. We get to elect the lesser judges, but the more important are appointed by governors or by the president with congressional confirmation.

The Constitution states that the president must appoint all federal judges and judges to the Supreme Court, district courts, and courts of appeal are appointed for life. There are federal courts in every state as well as in protectorates like Guam and Puerto Rico. The federal judges decide on matters with national consequences. Patents are litigated in federal courts as are tax matters, immigration, and matters that effect how states relate to each other. Federal courts also include military courts and courts dealing with special interests such as veterans. In 2000, the presidential race between George W. Bush and Al Gore was decided by the Supreme Court. Gore was the winner by popular vote, but he needed Florida's electoral votes to win the election. There was a state controversy on recounting ballots. The Supreme Court overruled a Florida court that ordered a recount of hand ballots. Without the recount, George Bush won the electoral votes and the presidency. Thus, the federal courts deal with issues that affect all Americans. Because these judges serve for life, their judicial philosophies vary with the president that appointed them. Some are liberal leaning (Democrats); some are conservative leaning (Republicans).

The county and state judges who need to be elected to office are nominated at the county nominating convention by members of the county Republican or Democratic committee. The people who want to run for a judgeship usually start visiting all of the town/city/village committees at their monthly meetings. Sitting judges seeking re-election are forbidden (by whom I do not know, but that is what they claim) from campaigning or participating in party politics except in the year of their election or re-election. Three judges showed up at our February party committee meeting, so I suspect that the election year starts in January for a November election. The judge candidates who appeared at the last committee meeting were each given a chance to speak to the committee (no citizens present) and all three said the same thing: I am not going to go over my credentials for this position, you know me. (I never saw any of them in my life.) Then they went on to brag about their participation in past party campaigns and how they held leadership positions in their respective towns and how they know that they can always count on our (town) committee to do the grunt work for their campaign -- (petitions, signs, door to door, brochures). Then they always have to leave to attend a committee meeting in another town.

The county convention sometimes allows judges and other candidates to give a three to five minute talk about why we should vote for them for the nomination. Most races have prearranged candidates and when a person's name is presented by a shill from the floor, the county party chair proposes a show of hands to make the person the party candidate by acclamation. When there are two or three candidates for an elected position, we committee people sometimes are allowed to vote by secret ballot for the one that we prefer. I suspect that the races for judges are fixed. At last year's convention, two people were seeking a family court judgeship. One candidate was a lawyer who had spent 10 years counseling delinquent children and negotiating family problems. The other was a lawyer who specialized in real estate closings, but was an officer of a town party. Needless to say, he got the nomination.

The county nominating conventions are in the spring of the year, so if two or more people are seeking a party nomination for a judgeship, the losers from the county convention can run a primary to challenge the choice of the convention. Of course, there is the little matter of getting 5% of the party voters in the area of the judgeship to sign petitions stating that they want this person to be the party candidate. A county judge candidate may need 5% of 200,000 voters to get a primary, and he or she has only 30 days to do this. This is how important it is to get the party nomination for a position.

The situation with town justice races is similar except that there is no nominating convention. Committee members are told who the candidate is. The party's executive committee makes the decision. In the old days, we were at least allowed to hear a five minute talk from each candidate. I will never forget one town justice race. We were offered two candidates to vote on. One candidate was a long-time town resident who had just retired from twenty years as the county's district attorney. He had a great reputation and impeccable credentials. His opponent was the son of the restaurant owner who used to give the party a free meeting room for our committee meetings. He was one year out of law school and did not know his name from page nine. Of course he won the "secret" ballot. Thus, I question "secret" ballots conducted by political parties. There are no monitors, no election inspectors, and I suspect that "secret" ballot means shred the pieces of paper that they collected and give the nomination to whom they were told to by the executive committee.

The election of judges is a problem for any democracy. However, there are a number of other groups involved in judgeships, the Bar Associations and the judge monitoring groups like the League of Women Voters. Local judges in larger municipalities are often endorsed or not by the local Bar Association. The intent is: who better knows a person's qualifications and judgment than his or her peers. Our local Bar Association has different levels of endorsement, such as, qualified, highly qualified, etc. Unfortunately, a Bar Association is no different than any other professional society. Lawyers sometimes attend meetings, sometimes not. Those that are active in the association may get a favorable endorsement, while those who do not participate may not get any endorsement simply because his or her peers do not know them as well as a person who regularly attends bar association functions.

The very best source of information on a judge's qualifications is from organizations like the League of Women Voters who sit in on trials and rate the judge's decisions. I have sat through many court cases awaiting my turn when I sue or get a traffic ticket and I have observed many differences in how judges, judge and run the court room. Many are fuss-budgets who demand all paperwork and procedures fit his or her rigid rules. They behave king-like. Others exude wisdom and judge-like demeanor. Some are good judges – some are not. Unfortunately, feedback on effectiveness in court is scarce. People with available time and persuasion to watch judges' behavior from the gallery are getting scarce. Thus, there is not an effective way to tell if a judge candidate is qualified and has the appropriate demeanor for the position sought. It is a crap-shoot for voters and that is a serious weakness of our democracy.

Strengths of America's Judge Selection Process

Lifetime appointments and ten-year terms go a long way in our democracy's keeping judges away from the influence of the people with campaign money. Town Justices often must run for re-election every two years. Needless to say, these people are susceptible to the great American flaw – favors in return for campaign contributions. Ten year terms allow those judges to be free of "campaign corruption" for about eight years of their ten-year term. Lifetime appointments completely eliminate the campaign contribution problem and that is a strength of our system. Some judge positions require candidates to be members in good standing with state bar, they must be "licensed" lawyers.

Some countries, like Iran, have judges appointed from the mullahs that control Islam. Some countries give judgeships (and control over laws) to friends and families. So the fact that most judgeships in America require a college degree and some demonstrated ability to deal with legal matters (passed the bar) is a strength of our system.

In addition, our media usually scrutinizes potential candidates to the point were criminals and people with low ethics are eliminated from the competition for judgeships. In general, most judicial candidates have the proper education and morality. Our ability to elect some of our judges ensures this. Congressional hearings on Supreme Court candidates seem to be a reasonable process for ferreting out candidates who may want to make laws rather than interpret them.

Weaknesses of Our Judge Selection System

A problem with our judicial system, besides no citizen input into who are made judges, is the litigious society that has evolved from bad judges. Judges who allow absurd claims, make judgments that no sane person would allow. They allow ambulance-chasing firms to become "suing industries." In every American city, the number of lawyers practicing is almost always more that the number of physicians. In my metropolitan area there are 10,730 lawyers in the phone book (nationwide, America has one lawyer for every eleven citizens), but just 3,200 physicians. We have more lawyers suing their neighbors, towns, and employees than we have physicians caring for our health. We used to have ads on TV for products that make life easier or pleasant or for recreation: new cars, boats, appliances, work-saving devices and products, etc. Now we only have ads from accident lawyers and pill companies. They are the only American "industries" with the cash needed to advertise. We have a system promoted by bad judges that allows one accident in a company to shut the company down. The most minor auto accident can cost an insurance company millions. People with no lasting injuries go on TV and give testimonials on how the ambulance chasing firm got him or her millions. These kinds of suits have made introducing really new products to Americans almost an impossibility. Entire industries in the US have ceased to exist because of the theft-through-court (TTC) system brought to us by bad judges, judges who know that the TTC lawyers are simply stealing from the deep-pocket targets that they have identified.

In addition to the judges who allow TTC, there are higher court judges that make their personal proclivities law. A judge with a fondness for birds can shut down entire regions of the country from all development activities because a group of birders thinks that the development will bother his or her favorite bird. In the 1990's, bad judges allowed the lawyers of the breast implant recipients who did not like their new cup size to shut down the implant industry. The asbestos lawsuits shut down the roofing industry and the automobile brake shoe industry. The bad judges have eliminated good paints for autos and machines because of claims that fumes from organic solvents kill people. Yet, the organic compounds (VOCs) emitted into the air by people fueling their own automobiles is at least a billion times more harmful to the atmosphere than solvent evaporation from paints. But the bad judges do not create "laws" to ban these VOCs because they do it themselves.

What we are alleging is that because of our lack of input into who can run our judicial system, America is becoming an impossible place to do business. Our judicial system has evolved from a constitutional watchdog and interpreter of laws into a "suing" industry that stifles business and makes our society one of the most litigious societies on earth. We do not talk with our neighbors: we sue them. In general, selecting judges is a weakness in our democracy that should be addressed.

Author's Commentary

Of course, we need judges to mediate trials, to decide competing issues in business, to sentence criminals, to decide on divorce and family matters, etc. What is not good for our society is that we are asked to elect (select) people that we know nothing about and could be poor decision-makers, incompetent, or even dishonest. How can Americans elect good judges without knowing them and their work? One thing that I would like to see from judicial candidates is curriculum vitae in place of flowery campaign literature. It would also be helpful if the news media would interview candidates for public offices. At the presidential appointment level, it would be helpful if all lifetime judge appointments be confirmed by congressional or state committees that are charged with supervision of our legal system.

Questions

1. Which judges are appointed for life, which do Americans get to vote for?
2. Who nominates candidates for judicial office?
3. Describe the primary process for judicial candidates.
4. Who monitors judges' decisions for corrections?
5. What are the terms of various judges?
6. What is the hierarchy of judges in America?
7. Which judge candidates campaign for office?
8. Who screens candidates for US Supreme Court judgeships?
9. What it TTC?
10. What can the average American citizen do to ensure a fair and competent judicial system?

Related Reading

1. Davis, Richard, <u>Electing Justice: Fixing the Supreme Court Nominating Process</u>, 2005.

2. Mallecorn, Kate, and Russell, Peter H., <u>Appointing Judges in an Age of Judicial Power: Critical Perspectives from Around the World</u>, 2006.

3. Chase, Harold W., <u>Federal Judges: The Appointing Process, Minnesota Archives Edition</u>, 1972.

4.   Epstein, Lee, and Segal, Jeffrey A., <u>Advice and Consent:</u>
        <u>The Politics of Judicial Appointment</u>, 2005.

Chapter 8

Our Government Departments, Agencies & Boards

Government agencies can be formed after a weekly meeting of a health department, government environmental department, a post office workers' meeting, any occasion can prompt a new government agency. In 2010, there was legislation pending in New York State to make walking while texting or listening to an iPod-type device against the law. Of course, if the law was passed an agency or department, etc. would have to be created to enforce the law. The state would have to hire mall watchers to arrest violations in shopping malls and then enforcers would be needed for street duty. Sounds ridiculous? In 1983, on a visit to Beijing China, we encountered spitting police on every block of every street. It was against the law to spit in public and the "city government" hired people to widely enforce the law with tickets that required a fine. We have jay-walking laws that are similar, but not widely enforced.

Laws and regulations require enforcement and this means an agency, board, police, etc. and its accompanying bureaucracy. This is a product of governments who believe that they need to modify the behavior of its citizens. America's democracy is mired in behavior-modification agencies, boards, and assorted other entities to make their citizen behave to the government's liking.

Of course, there are good reasons for some of this. Jay-walking kills people. Spitting is a filthy habit that is disgusting to viewers and spreads disease. Walking while texting can lead to injury on colliding with fixed objects. How far should a government go to protect its citizens from themselves?

Government departments and agencies operate within organization charts, but often they can assume powers that affect constitutional rights. For example, in my city, the city council voted to give the city building inspectors the right to enter any rental property at any time without due process or warrant to inspect for code violations. The 4th amendment to the Constitution states, "The right of the people to be secure in their persons, houses, papers, and effects, against unreasonable searches and seizures, shall not be violated, and no Warrants shall issue, but upon probable cause, supported by Oath or affirmation, and particularly describing the place to be searched, and the persons or things to be seized."

My city also has a health department that decided that lead paint in old houses was causing lead poisoning in children and they obtained laws from the city legislature that requires people who buy a house built before the ban of lead paints (1973) to remove or cover all lead paint using a city certified lead abatement company. Essentially, this edict from a city department makes 98% of the housing stock in the city unsellable. Again, a violation of the Bill of Rights.

At the town level, many towns have instituted planning and zoning agencies. Most of these government bodies consist of six to ten members appointed by the town council. Appointments are usually made by the town supervisor with approval of the town council. These boards have tremendous power. They can stop landowners from using their land; they can apply requirements that make it impossible to improve a property; they have complete control over use of land and structures that people buy and the citizenry has no choice in the designation of the people who make up these boards or any say in construction or land use in "their" town. As an example, A local developer bought several acres of worthless swamp area that had been an eyesore for decades with the intent of building upscale apartments. Then without so much as a notice to the property owner, the local department of environmental conservation posted no-trespassing signs on his property, not allowing even him on his property. Apparently, a trespasser noticed an eagle nesting in a tree and this allowed the environmental agency to take over the property without compensation or due process of law. There are agencies in government who assume powers incommensurate with the Constitution.

At the state level, the environmental departments often usurp America's Constitution. In the Florida Keys, waterfront properties cannot cut mangrove growth blocking their view of the ocean. In my neighborhood, the state environmental office shut down a 300-boat marina because the marina operator was keeping the harbor channel open by using propeller wash from a workboat. They said that blowing sand from the natural channel hurts the environment, even though sand to a depth of two feet moves into the harbor entrance in every northeast storm and then out with the predominantly west wind. The same state organization said nothing as a hydro facility raised the level in one of the Great Lakes 1 ½ feet above the highest tolerable level and wiped out hundreds of miles of beaches.

Strengths of America's Governmental Agencies

America has an agency/board/council – whatever to control every aspect of activity, every aspect of life of every citizen. Each one of these agencies was formed to address some evil or problem. A county will have a clerk for records, an emergency organization, an environmental organization, a water department, a transportation department, a medical examiner, a motor vehicle bureau, a court system, a prosecutor, a social services (welfare) office, a Social Security office, an education department, an election commission, an animal control function, as well as police and fire protection services.

Most of these departments are duplicated at the state level along with additional agencies like consumer protection, tourist services, hunting and fishing permits, taxation, a comptroller or treasury department, plus their court system.

At the federal level, we add customs, border protection, FBI, post office, OSHA, military recruiting, the coast guard, education department, Internal Revenue, Veterans Affairs, NOAA, etc. We have agencies for everything. If a citizen of the US has any problem that is in any way related to government, there is an agency that a citizen can go to for help. Similarly, we do not have to be concerned about how to protect our house from fires. There are government organizations who specify what we must do (smoke alarms, fire escapes, sprinklers, etc.). We do not have to worry about having our vehicle hit by an uninsured driver. There are agencies that make sure all autos are insured. We do not need to worry about our children's education. There are government agencies that ensure that every child in America is given a good education. We do not need to fight for improved highways; there is a government entity to plan and build necessary roads.

There is not one aspect of life that is not guided by a government agency and it is their purpose to make life better for every American citizen. We do not need to worry about anything.

Weakness of Our Government Agencies

Our examples of how government departments and agencies make "laws" that are not supported by America's Constitution and certainly not by her citizens. There is no consensus; they are not democratic; they evolved from governments reacting to incidents. That is a crushing failure of America's democracy. Every time that there is an incident or lobby effort by a special interest group, America's government reacts with ill-conceived laws, departments, boards, agencies, and the like. Automobile licensing costs taxpayers maybe 40 billion dollars a year and millions of hours of citizen time. Auto licensing started in the early 20th century as a way to inhibit car theft. It has not done that yet. American citizens have to pay dearly for this government program that could be replaced by a unique number applied to a vehicle at manufacture. This could be your auto license.

Author's Commentary

The solution to the plethora of agencies, boards, commissions, and the like that have assumed "unconstitutional" powers, needs to be addressed at every government level. America's democracy needs to have an appeal function that pertains to every code, law, and mandate that usurps a citizen's freedom, property, business, etc. The appeal should be heard first by the agency that imposed the "eagle rule" then another appeal should be allowed to a jury of ordinary citizens.

I commiserate with the developer with the eagle problem. I have a problem with beavers destroying large mature trees on the golf course that I play on. They made an absolute mess – destroyed 50 and 100 year-old trees. They were too big to fell. They girdled them and they died. Each removal would cost about $10,000. The town animal control agency said that they have a trapper who would trap the offending animals free of charge to the taxpayers, but the environmental conservation agency said that these rodents are protected by some law and they must be permitted to continue to destroy private property and ruin a golf business.

There are countless stories like mine all over the country – government agencies assume unconstitutional powers and we citizens have no redress. Unfair tax assessments are another example. Maybe we need a constitutional amendment like:

> *No government agency or government*
> *employee shall make laws, decisions,*
> *or mandates that deny citizens rights*
> *guaranteed by the Constitution*

Questions

1. Name the Federal agency responsible for interstate highways.

2.   Name a government department that exists at the county, state, and federal levels.
3.   Who initiates federal agencies?
4.   Who initiates state agencies?
5.   Name three federal agencies.
6.   Name three state agencies.
7.   How can agencies or boards be terminated?
8.   Name three agencies controlled by the President.
9.   What is the mechanism for citizen input to boards and agencies.
10.   How would you use a government agency – give an example.

Related Reading

1.   Wilson, James Q., <u>Bureaucracy: What Agencies do and Why They do it</u>, 1991.

2.   Bardoch, Eugene, <u>Getting Agencies to Work Together: The Practice and Theory of Managed Craftsmanship</u>.

3.   <u>US Department of State Handbook</u>: US Government Agencies Investment and Business Library), Ibp USA on USA International publications, 2000.

Chapter 9

Our Government Authorities

Authorities were created by various American government entities to address a specific task/facility/infrastructure/highway that is in the public interest. Any municipality or state government can create an authority. It is not known to me what part of the Constitution allows authorities, but there appears to be absolutely no controls on these organizations other than state and local legislatures. If some government official decides that he or she would like some extra discretionary funds, not obtained by traditional taxes, he or she can have the state or municipal legislature create an authority such as, to create electricity from Niagara Falls and sell it to make money for the authority. The authority is run by people selected by the person creating the authority – a board of directors appointed by the authority originator and confirmed by the pertinent legislature. The authority sells bonds to fund the project and the authority decides what to do with the proceeds. Of course, the proceeds pay the debt service on the bonds, the salaries of board members, and whatever is left is discretionary income for the "owner" of the authority. In the Niagara Falls example, the authority that built a huge facility to harness hydro power from Niagara Falls is called the New York State Power Authority. They built hydro plants at Niagara Falls, Messina, and other places around the State of New York and they have a surplus of billions of dollars a year that the New York State Governor, the creator and "owner" of the authority can use for any purpose he or she deems necessary. One example of where the NY Power Authority has spent its excess revenue is to subsidize power to selected (by the governor) industries or municipalities. For example, 15% of the power from the dam that controls the water flow from the Great Lakes goes to the Alcoa Aluminum Refinery in Messina, NY. Villages that have their own electric distribution system get NY Power Authority power at $.02/kw while all others in the state pay more than $.10/kw.

The only east-west interstate highway through New York State, the NYS Thruway, US 90, was built by the NYS Thruway Authority in the 1950's. The Thruway Authority charges a toll to pay for the road and repairs. Well, the road was paid for decades ago and now the Thruway revenue is another cash cow for discretionary spending by the governor. In the last 20 years or so, the authority bought the state prisons for a few billion dollars to balance the governor's budget. Another time they bought the Erie Canal to give the state some more billions to pay for state employee raises. In 2008, the Thruway Authority was using its revenues to pay the salaries of thousands of friends and relatives to hand out tickets to vehicles entering the Thruway, even though all other states have "take-a-ticket" machines.

On the local scene, our city has a sports authority that built a baseball stadium for 30M, a soccer stadium for 25M, and they are trying to find a Lacrosse team so they can build a stadium for one if they find one. Of course, the baseball and soccer stadiums lose money and require an annual operating subsidy from the county legislature as well as money to pay for the stadium debt. Also, the teams are losers and nobody attends the games. However, our stadiums are not as egregious as the 100,000-seat football stadium in San Antonio built by their sports authority at a cost of hundreds of millions of dollars. They do not have a football team. They wanted one, but the American Football League decided that they were too close to the Houston franchise, and thus, did not warrant a team of their own. I asked a cab driver, "What do you do with it?" He said "high-school football tournaments are played there in front of several hundred fans."

At the town level, the town where I own property was given several hundred acres by a failing industry who could no longer afford the town's outrageous property taxes. Much of the land abutted a busy US highway so the town, rather than use it for park or green space like the company wanted, rented the land to typical American fast-food franchises. They created several authorities to do the leasing and take the money. The members of the authorities and mostly town employees and there is no public accounting of what happens to the money. How much do these employees get for being board members, what expenses do they claim, etc. The town budget shows a solitary entry of $5,000 etc. from "authorities." I suspect that the annual leases bring in millions, but we citizens will never know. It is not a concern that town government who make the building laws is competing with private land owners who would love to rent to Olive Garden, but cannot get through the town's approval thicket.

The ultimate local authority, the example that transcends even the taking of America from Native American's is our county water authority. This "authority" built a water treatment plant and stuck a pipe into a lake to get water to sell to the county residents. No matter that the city already had a wonderful system in place including its own pristine lake 30 miles away and a huge reservoir on the highest piece of land in the area. Well, the water authority sold their water to the suburbs that were growing in the 60's and after. They became very wealthy from our quarterly water bills and handsomely paid the authority members as well as their employees. Since the county legislature has been controlled by the Republican Party for decades, they had control of the water authority and its lucrative salaries. So, if a Republican politician lost on election and needed a job, he or she found one at the water authority; our county manager's husband lost his job. No problem, he found a great job at the water authority. This business was so good and so vital to the owning political party that in 2008, they decided to grow the business. The legislature approved $200 million in bonds to build another not-needed plant several miles to the west. Republicans can also be entrepreneurs.

In summary, authorities are a contemporary addition to America's government powers. They allow governments to build huge capital projects without voter approval. They are a government business often in competition with free enterprise. They can spring up after a political leader lunch and they can saddle taxpayers for huge debt for decades into the future. There appears to be no way for American's citizens to curtail use of authorities to circumvent citizen approval of projects.

Strengths of America's Authorities

Most American citizens want capital projects for the common good. Most Americans agree with the concept of authorities: they do things without additional taxes. The users of the capital project pay for the project. The Blue Water Bridge which joins Michigan to Ontario Canada was a huge project – hundreds of millions of dollars in the 1950's. It saved hundreds of miles for people traveling from the Toronto population center to Chicago and Michigan destinations. The bridge toll paid for the project. The bridge was paid for in 30 years with ample funds for upkeep. However, after 60 years, the tolls are much higher than when the bridge was being built. So what happens to this windfall? The governor of Michigan can use these funds for any purpose he or she deems necessary.

Besides allowing significant capital projects to be user-funded, authorities allow projects in regions of "stingy" residents. There are many towns, cities, and villages in America with high percentages of retirees. These citizens have fixed incomes and would reject any capital improvement that increases their taxes in any way. They may not approve fixing potholes in roads if it cost them more taxes. Authorities can solve his problem. Voter approval is not needed. An authority only needs approval of the legislative body in entity. In a town or village, this may mean only four people. It is not necessary to sell citizenry on needed projects.

Weaknesses of America's Authorities

So what's wrong with America's authorities? They are our fastest growing government entity. Their concept is infinitely simple: (1) decide to build something, (2) issue bonds to pay for it, (3) pay for the "something" with the revenues brought in by the project. Well, firstly, when the project does not bring in enough money to pay down the debt, the taxpayers hold the bag (like our loser stadiums). Secondly, but most important, taxpayers have no say in if they want the project. It is how municipalities build things that they know for sure that the taxpayers would reject if they were asked. Then there is the corruption that is systemic to authorities. The "members" of the authorities are not ordinary citizens; they are not elected; they are not often approved by any legislative body; they are friends and relatives, retired politicians and assorted other bottom feeders that have spent their lives living off taxpayer dollars. Finally, there is the constitutionality of authorities. Does any American believe that the founding fathers drafted a constitution that would promote spending taxpayer monies in projects that the people may not want, but are never asked about? I think not.

Author's Commentary

Authorities definitely need some form of citizen control. At present, they have none. Four elected officials can meet and decide to build a Lacrosse stadium for 50 million dollars. They have the town/city/village/county lawyers draw up the necessary paperwork for selling bonds to get the money. The law firm markets the bonds (and takes their cut) and they start building. Then the taxpayers are told that they are getting this new stadium and it will bring in millions of dollars a month in tourist dollars and will entice America's best young people to move to the area. This is the standard format. Taxpayers are never, never asked if they want or see a need for a Lacrosse stadium and this action is definitely incongruent with the principals of democracy, but has been made legal by lawyers and others in government who benefit from such things, and they must forever pay for losses and upkeep of the unwanted stadium.

What can be done to reign in "authority mania" in the US? This may be number one on the list of constitutional amendments needed. A suitable amendment might read:

*"No 'authority' or other entity in government
shall initiate and carry out capital projects for
the common good without a voter referendum from
the concerned portion of the country. A capital project
is defined as new building or work costing over
$1,000,000
in 2010. This definition shall be reviewed by Congress
every 3 years.*

*Authority board members shall serve without
remuneration except for expenses and all authorities are to be
abolished at the completion of the capital project. Thereon the
project shall be transferred in perpetuity to the government
organization that initiated the authority."*

*We definitely need some protection like this. The
concept of forcing huge projects on citizens who have no say in
the project, but must pay for them is certainly not what the
founding fathers had in mind.*

Questions

1. What is an authority?
2. What branch of government can create an authority?
3. How do authorities work?
4. How is an authority ended?
5. How does one get a job on an authority?
6. What is wrong with using an authority to build a sports stadium?
7. Who audits authorities?
8. How are capital projects normally funded by a county government?
9. Who buys the bonds that authorities sell for their projects?
10. How can authorities be curtailed?

Related Reading

1.   VanFleet, Alanson A., <u>The Tennessee Valley Authority</u>, 1981.

2.   Elcock, H., <u>Local Government: Policy and Management in Local Authorities</u>, 1994.

3.   Mitchell, Jerry, <u>Public Authorities and Public Policy: The Business of Government</u>, 1992.

4.   Axelrod, Donald, <u>Shadow Government: The Hidden World of Public Authorities and How They Control Over $1 Trillion of Your Money</u>, 1992.

Chapter 10

Our Government Research and Development

America's contribution to scientific knowledge comes from research funding from America's military and government departments, notably the Department of Energy, the Department of Transportation, and the National Science Foundation (NSF), the FDA (Health Department, Center for Disease Control, National Institutes of Health, NASA and minor funding from other federal agencies. The national laboratories: NIST, Brookhaven, Argonne, Oak Ridge, Los Alamos, Sandia, Jet Propulsion, etc. are government-funded research facilities. The following are comments on the research that we are aware of in some of these areas.

National Science Foundation (NSF)

Overall, NSF is America's principle source of funding for academic research. NSF grants to universities pay the tuition and fees for most of the Masters and Ph.D. degrees awarded in the sciences. Their funding in 2008 was about $6B and this constitutes 20% of the $30B that the USA allotted to basic research in 2008 through all departments. The way that NSF functions is that they accept proposals for research from academic institutions and sometimes businesses; they have a review process and then fund some of the proposals (40,000 proposals in 2008, 10,000 were funded). The usual product of the research is a published paper and a graduated Ph.D. To a significant degree, they "supply" our science professors in universities

The National Labs

The National Labs provide the United State's with in-house research and development. They were managed by a "hired" commercial research organization in 2010. They have been managed by other companies such as airplane manufacturers. Each lab has different capabilities and specialties. For example, Oak Ridge National Lab in Tennessee is famous as the birthplace of the atomic bomb that ended World War II. They still have a significant nuclear activity along with their non-nuclear research. The Jet Propulsion Lab in California is noted for their prowess in space related technologies. Sandia National Lab in 2011 had a strong emphasis in electronics. Argonne National Lab ins 2010 did significant research in engineering materials and coatings.

The National Institute for Standards and Technology was established as the National Bureau of Standards (NBS) in the early part of the 1900's. It was located in Washington, D.C. and its purpose was to be a reference on weights and measures – they defined "a pound," "a meter," a degree Fahrenheit," etc. Since World War II, they delved into many non-measure areas to the point where their name was changed to NIST to reflect their broad research effort. They still supply industry with standard reference materials and measurement guidance, but this is not their only area of responsibility.

Military Research

The Naval Research Lab in Washington, D.C. was started in about 1890 to do research on naval weaponry, and they later became the technology center for the Navy's nuclear-powered vessels. They do a wide variety of research, but much of it is ultimately directed at problems associated with naval warfare.

The Army has many labs researching the things that pertain to ground warfare. For example, the research materials for armor, cannons, missiles, and the like. They also do the research for military vehicles and communications.

The Air Force has a very large research facility at Wright Patterson Air Force Base in Dayton and there they do research related to flight and aerial warfare. They can test materials for propellers, helicopter rotors, jet engines, and aircraft bodies.

Medical Health Research

There are a variety of federal agencies that deal with health and medical issues. The Food and Drug Administration has the responsibility for approving all of the drugs that we are allowed to take, medical devices, the safety of food, radiation safety and the like. This agency, above all others, has a direct influence on every American in reference to what drugs they allow us to ingest. Some people in the medical industry believe that the organization should be split into two – one for food safety, and one for medical health issues. The impetus for such a change being improved response in approving new drugs and medical devices. Approval by any government organization in any matter is usually lethargic simply because of the serious risks of "wrong approvals." Besides approval of new drugs, medical procedures, and devices, the FDA has research dollars that it can apply to research in the areas included in their responsibility.

The Institutes of Health is also under the US Department of Health and Human Services and they annually invest billions of dollars in health research, mostly to universities and research institutes. They have been functioning for more that 50 years and they claim that their research has solved many health problems. Also, under the Department of Health and Human Services is the US Centers for Disease Control which works on controlling diseases such as swine flu which became a pandemic on 2009.

Overall, the US Federal government is the largest source of funding for research into many of the factors and businesses that control our lives. The positive aspect of this is that research dollars are widely available to universities and other researchers.

Strengths of America's R&D

America's foremost strength may be the amount of R&D compared to the competition. Besides the National Labs, NSF, and NIST, many Federal and State entities sponsor research and development. Some states spend in excess of 100 million dollars per year through their universities and other R&D entities. Many counties and cities have business incubators that allow R&D to produce products that people buy and jobs that people need.

Our military R&D probably makes our military the most technically advanced in the world. In 2010, America waged a very active aerial war in the Afghanistan/Pakistan border region by drones controlled by military personnel in a bunker some place in the mountains of Colorado.

Our space research is probably the most advanced on our planet and America's space-related R&D activities have given the world many important new materials for other applications. The high-strength, high-toughness steel developed for aerospace applications are now widely used to improve the service life of manufacturing equipment.

American's medical research which is highly sponsored by government has brought its citizens incredible advances in medical devices. Arthroscopic surgery and robotic surgery (DaVinci, etc.) allow less invasive operations and better success rates for many health problems. Vaccines developed by America's R&D have ended a wide variety of diseases as problems to our citizenry. We no longer worry about polio, tuberculoses, measles, yellow fever, bubonic plaque and the like that still ravage parts of our planet.

Overall, America's R&D has been mostly money well spent. We have made it part of what a government does, part of the common good.

Weakness of America's R&D

Government funded R&D is a necessary part of our democracy. It supplies the funds to produce our Ph.D.'s – our teachers, our learned people, our researchers. The problem that exists is that our young and talented minds are told what to work on. They only work on things that are likely to get funded and bureaucrats who have no science, industrial, educational, medical, or public sector background make the decisions on what gets funded. Funding also changes with presidencies and leadership in other government levels.

From 2002 to 2008, America's government spent countless billions of tax dollars researching fuel cells for automobiles and household energy production. Then there was a presidential change and a new person was appointed to head the Department of Energy. That person personally did not believe in fuel cells, so the entire effort was shut down and the funding stopped. We will never know if fuel cells could have helped solve our energy and air problems, but competing countries like China may now be free to corner the market and preclude America's use of this technology.

As I write this, America's return to the moon research has been shut down by Washington bureaucrats. Countless billions and decades of work were halted. It will even cost about three billion dollars to shut down the program. The reason given for the shut down – we already did it. Let's go someplace else. No matter that the moon may have huge resources of critical metals that our planet is running out of. Some are critical elements predicted to be totally exhausted by 2020. For example, we cannot have any of the electronic devices that now control our planet when critical conductor metals, copper and gold, run out. We already are experiencing the cost of limited gold supply (over $1,000/ounce) and copper is predicted to be exhausted by 2050. America must fund research at universities if we are to have scientists and educators in significant number/Ph.D's are government funded. An obvious problem with government-funded research is what to work on. The

President can dictate what the national labs, like Oak Ridge, will work on. Of course, national labs are appropriate choices for research on military projects, but overall, America's citizens have no input into how their R&D tax dollars are used.

Author's Commentary

If the average American was asked what American's obtained from government research, it is likely that most could not mention one example. Some people may remember the atomic bomb and nuclear subs, but most would have no idea as the what benefits they obtained from the thirty billion or so dollars that America spends on research and development each year. So the government organizations that fund research should make an effort to let America's citizens know what they got for their money.

Conversely, it would be ethical and appeasing to Americans to query them occasionally on what they think should be researched by our government. For example, the following is one taxpayers (moi) top ten list of things that need research.

1. *Creation of sustainable jobs for all Americans who want to work*
2. *Develop sustainable ways of generating electricity*
3. *Develop practical zero-heat and zero-air conditioned houses for less cost than current stick-built houses*
4. *Develop vaccines for colon, prostate, and breast cancers*
5. *Develop sustainable and green personal transport vehicles*
6. *Permanent highways (require no maintenance after building)*
7. *Low cost, practical energy from human, animal, and food waste*

8.   Develop computers that can be programmed to do useful control functions by spoken or typed commands

9.   Failure-free electricity production

10.   Food crops that can be grown anywhere

Every American would have a different list, but lists such as this could be presented to Americans occasionally to get their input. Americans are not as stupid as elected officials deem. If offered the opportunity, we can help run the country. Polling on research priorities can be done very easily on the internet. Americans vote by the millions on who danced the best. Why not ask them where their research dollars should be spent.

Currently, for too much of our research investment is squandered on issues that have little bearing on the common good. Also, too much of government research is redundant. In 2010, every state and every national lab has an effort in nanotechnology. It is currently trendy. Twenty years ago, it was superconductivity. Next it will be sustainability or the like. Somebody not in government needs to police the entire government effort to prevent duplication.

Questions

1.   What is government funded research?
2.   Where is government funded research done?
3.   What is the role of NIST?
4.   What is the role of America's national Labs in research?
5.   How is government research funded?
6.   What does the FDA do?
7.   What does the CDC do?
8.   What government agency researches conversion to wind energy?
9.   Where is military research done?
10.   Where is space research done?

Related Reading

1.   Westwick, Peter J., <u>The National Labs: Science in an American System</u>, 2003.

2.   Hawthorn, Fran, <u>Inside the FDA: The business and Politics Behind the Drugs We Take and The food We Eat</u>, 2005.

3.   Richards, Byron J., <u>Fight for Your Health: Exposing the FDA's Betrayal of America</u>, 2006.

4.   Hills, Philip J., <u>Protecting America's Health: The FDA Business, and One Hundred Years of Regulation</u>, 2004

5.   Smith, Kevin B., <u>State and Local Government</u>, 2010-2011Edition.

Chapter 11

Funding Election Campaigns

America's democracy costs a lot of money. The 2008 presidential campaign cost hundreds of millions of dollars. President Obama's 2012 re-election campaign is predicted to cost at least one billion dollars. The House of Representative races cost about 500 million dollars in 2008. Most of these moneys are for advertising and the rest is for campaign staff and travel. Where does this money come from? A small portion of the 10 to 12 billion that a general election costs come from ordinary citizens interested in their democracy. However, most of it comes from people and organizations who want something in return for their "contribution."

Unions

Labor unions are by far the largest contributors to political candidates (95% of union contributions go to the Democratic Party). Unions eventually tax their members for funds to support union officers and to lobby governments to make laws that give them more power, more membership, and more ability to increase the wages of their membership. The mission of unions is not the common good; to the contrary, their mission is to increase the wealth and well-being of their members. They usually do this with complete and absolute deference to the effect of their demands on the general public.

What makes union control of elections so devastating to America's democracy is that most public sector employees are unionized. About one third of tax-paying Americans work for the Government. This includes school teachers and school employees, and suppliers to educational institutions. Teacher unions, health care workers, highway workers, postal workers, many times tithe to the union to lobby for their pay and benefits and to contribute to political candidates who will continue to increase their pay and benefits. Unfortunately, the private sector has no one lobbying or contributing to candidates who are not beholding to unions.

Pig Roasts

Every political committee in America annually conducts a pig roast or some other event to raise funds. These events are attended by quid pro quo business interests and public employees interested in sucking up to the politician who the event is for. There are different hierarchies to pig roasts. The town committee raises tens of thousands of dollars to support town-wide candidates. County-wide pig roasts are expected to raise from 0.5 M to tens of millions. State events even more. Then there are national fund raisers. My brother-in-law, the banking executive, paid (from company funds) $5,000 to have his photo taken with a president running for reelection. It took only 30 seconds (that's $600,000 for an hour shoot – not bad money). All of the people who pay more than market rate for a pig roast ($19.95 including coffee) are contributing to get their name or their company's name on a list of contributors who expect something in return.

The Rich and Famous

Another significant source of funding for America's elections is the very rich and the famous (and rich) people like movie and stage stars. The latter often do not have to contribute any of their money. For example, hundreds of people from the Communist Party would probably pay $1,000 for a cocktail party attended by Jane Fonda. It only costs her a few hours away from her tweeting with her North Korean friends.

The billionaire types can buy elections, can overthrow some foreign governments, run their own political parties, buy entire towns, etc. Mit Romney reportedly spent $40 M of his own money for his unsuccessful bid to be the Republican Presidential candidate on 2008. Ross Perot bought 12% of the vote in his 1990 presidential bid. One billionaire in 2009 offered all statewide candidates for office a million dollars for their election campaign if they signed a survey and proposed a method for accountability once elected. He had no takers, but this shows the power that the rich and famous have over who runs for office and who wins. Candidates in America do win any election unless his or her name is known by the electorate and getting "known" costs money.

Companies and Businesses

People and organizations who want government business or legislation favorable to a business or industry are probably the most significant "funders" of political candidates. Of course, the candidate knows that and still takes the money because there is never too much money for campaigns. The higher the office, the more likely businesses will be there with open checkbooks, free private plane rides and Super Bowl tickets. There are some states that have laws limiting "favors" to candidates, but it still happens and it is a significant failing of our system.

Recognition is all important in American polities. Notoriety is as good as paid publicity. There is no bad publicity. A mayor of D.C. was accused of a wide variety of crimes, yet he kept winning reelection. People felt that they "knew" him and they could accept his alleged faults in preference to taking a chance on a person who they were not familiar with. The current method of election funding unquestionably compromises the integrity of candidates and give us a democracy that is a product of special interests. How should democratic elections be funded? Differently than at present.

Strengths of America's Election Campaign System

America's present election campaign system is a personification of free enterprise – anything goes. A candidate can spend any amount of money. In lots of cases, the amount spent can be significant per person. In 2011, a candidate for

mayor of Chicago spent $12 million dollars on his campaign –
more than $10 for each vote.

Every candidate can raise as much money as he or she
wants. There are election laws that put some limits on amounts
that corporations can give to candidates, but political action
committees and similar "devices" are used to bypass most
contribution restrictions.

Our extensive campaigning system gives America's
citizens a better opportunity to get to know candidates for office.
For example, presidential contenders often start the campaigns
two years before the conventions that select the presidential
candidates. Certain states like New Hampshire have early events
that draw the contenders who decide early to run.

At the local level, the "pig roasts" give all citizens an
opportunity to mingle and get to know candidates for a moderate
contribution. The need for continuing campaign contributions
also prompts elected officials to establish "breakfast clubs" and
other groups of citizens to get contributions and allow citizens to
give their input to elected officials on their concerns. A senator
is more likely to listen to a single citizen at a "chat session" than
from a letter sent to his or her office. Letters are usually
screened so that maybe one in 100 will be read by the elected
official. Thus, there are some citizen benefits from our extensive
campaigning system.

Weaknesses of America's Election Campaign System

It is fundamentally wrong for unions to fund campaigns
for elected office. Belonging to a union should not take away a
US citizen's party choice. For the last 20 years, all unions in the
US mandated that their members register and vote Democratic.
It is fundamentally wrong for rich people to spend five or 100
million dollars to "buy" elected offices as a billionaire did in
New York City. Our "anything goes" system clearly makes the
rich best positioned to run for elected office. In fact, at most
every level of government in the US, the current elected officials

are financially independent to rich. Very few elected members of government at any level are full-time mechanics at the local Chevy dealership. The very foundation of our democracy: all people have access to public office; has been compromised. Essentially, only the rich and public employees can run for elected office.

Our smartest, most available, and wisest citizens may have ordinary jobs with the usual family-related economic issues (tuition, taxes, etc.) and thus they cannot jeopardize their jobs with an election campaign that requires daily travel, speeches during working hours, and the like. In fact, job concerns probably preclude participation in elected office for most Americans. This is fundamentally wrong.

Author's Commentary

America has more than 230 years of funding of candidates for elected office by entities seeking favors. The UK has addressed this issue in their parliamentary democracy. Campaign contributions from all sources are limited to about 10,000 Pounds per candidate for members of parliament races. This is the kind of bold step America needs. When running for the lowest level of congress, representatives, costs $500,000 minimum, it is time to put the brakes on. Ordinary people cannot participate in America's government and our government becomes controlled by special interests. America has this situation in 2010 with labor unions, contributing disproportionately to election campaigns. Unions were never permitted in the public sector for most of America's history. John Kennedy allowed them and now public employee unions can often control elections with their campaign contributions. This is a problem that should be addressed. Campaign spending limits like the UK also be instituted. We cannot have a participatory government that costs tens of thousands to millions of dollars to participate in.

Without question, the most significant fault in America's democracy is campaign donations from special interest groups.

The only way to give all American's an equal opportunity to seek elected office would be to eliminate the 5% petition requirement that prohibits 99% of all interested candidates from running for office, and totally ban all monetary and contributions in kind in all elections in America. Of course, candidates would not be allowed to spend their own wealth because that would not be fair. So individuals running for office could not spend more than some nominal amount – like $300.00 and each candidate for office would have to have 20 signatures or 1% of the voters, whichever is greater for the area in which they are running.

Citizens could get to "know" the candidates through government-arranged and funded talks. Public television in localities would be encouraged to give each local candidate five minutes for their pitch three times within two months of an election. There would also be local, state, and federal funded websites that would give each candidate two pages. Presidential elections could be funded only by the dollar income tax donations. Any citizen who has a fervor to support a candidate could do so by posting signs that he or she pays for on their property or on their vehicle as long as their support does not cost more than $100.00 or some nominal amount.

Questions

1. What is the spending limit for federal, state, country, town, and village election campaigns?
2. What is a lobbyist and what do they do for a living?
3. What group/entity spends the most for lobbying in the USA?
4. What is the limit that companies and organizations can contribute to election campaigns?
5. Who enforces limits on campaign spending?
6. How can a wealthy person or organization "buy" and elected office?
7. What happens to unspent campaign funds?
8. Why is it wrong for public employees to be allowed to form unions?

9.   What can be done to control the costs of election
        campaigns?
10.   What is the effect of unlimited campaign spending for
        elected office?

Related Reading

1.   Palda, K. Fitys, <u>How Much is Your Vote Worth: The
        Unfairness of Campaign Spending Limits</u>, 1993.

2.   Johnson, R.J., <u>Money and Votes Constituency Campaign
        Spending and Election Results</u>, 1987.

3.   Kahn, Kim Fridkin, and Kenney, Patrick J., <u>The
        Spectacle of US Senate Campaigns</u>, 1999.

4.   Nassmacher, Karl-Heinz, Zovotto, Daniel, Ballington,
        Julie, and Austin, Reg, <u>Funding of Parties and Election
        Campaigns: A Handbook</u>, 2003.

5.   Ewing, Keith, Tham, Joo Cheong, and Rawbottom,
        Jacob, <u>The Funding of Political Parties: Where Now?</u>,
        2011.

Chapter 12

What It Means to be a Republican or Democrat

A requirement of America's democracy is only two competing groups of citizens for every elected office. Of course, America has many political parties; some arise for specific issues, some, like the Communist party, have been on the scene for decades, but because of their small size, they are usually irrelevant when it comes to elected office. At least 99.9% of all elected officials in America are registered members of the Democratic or Republican Party. Once people officially register with a state election commission as a Democrat or Republican, they then have those labels. Those who opt not to be one of these, but still register with the election commission to vote are listed as independents or members of some other minor parties that are not usually strong enough in an area to have a place on the ballot.

Some states have Liberal, Conservative, Right-to-Life, Working person party, and Communist party on the ballot. As mentioned previously, the minor parties do not have enough members and organization to field candidates for most available elected offices, so most voters do not subscribe to these parties because they know that their vote will be wasted. It will not go for one of the two people who will win the election. This may not be right, but this is the situation in America in 2008.

What constitutes a Republican and a Democrat? The simple answer is a Democrat is a registered voter in the Democratic Party; a Republican is a voter registered in the Republican Party. But why do different people select one or the other party?

The Republican Party

At the start of our democracy, George Washington was liked by all but the Continental Congress that developed the Constitution and the citizenry consisted of two distinct groups: (1) Those who made their living in agriculture (90% of the population), and (2) Those who lived in cities and made their living in city things such as retail, commerce, shipping, finance (10% of the population). The former were called Democratic Republicans, the latter Federalists. Thus, early on, the parties represented differing economic interests; one farming, one city living.

In the first half of the 19th century, slavery was a big part of the agriculture business, especially in the south. Slaves did much of the plantation work. Eventually, slavery became a defining factor in the two-party system. Those who favored slavery (and agriculture) were represented by what became the Democratic Party, and those who wanted abolition of slavery became represented by what became the Republican Party. Abraham Lincoln was the first president identified as a member of the Republican Party. The Civil War under Lincoln polarized the country into more than two political parties. People were either for the Union Army under Lincoln and the Republican Party or the Confederates who wanted, not only to be a single political party, but they wanted to be a separate country – the Confederate States of America.

We all know what happened, but the country went back to the original democracy norm with two political parties, the Democrats and the Republicans. The South was almost completely Democratic and the remainder of the healing country was a mix of Republicans and Democrats. Eventually, all states in the union tended toward a preference of one or the other party. The Republican philosophy continued to be that government should be only as big as needed to do the job, and people will provide for their own well being if the government leaves them alone. Their platforms usually call for no new taxes, a strong military, and traditional values.

The Democratic Party

The industrial revolution in the late 19th century brought people from the farms to the cities. The cities needed lots of people to run them; the factories needed lots of people to run them. Factories started to exploit people and so did cities. Unions were a result of workers' response. The factories were headed by Republicans – self-reliant entrepreneurs. The factories and cities were staffed by exploited people. They unionized and unions became the basis of the Democratic Party. The party philosophy evolved along the lines that government can best control the welfare of the citizenry. The Democrats created a plethora of agencies to ensure the welfare of the citizenry. America was on the rocks in the 1930's or thereabouts because of the Great Depression. Franklin Delano Roosevelt was elected as the Democratic President in 1932 and he started to restore the country by government make-work projects like parks, reservoirs, bridges, etc. He instituted social programs such as Social Security, all kinds of things to provide work (jobs) for the people. He restored America, and that is why city dwellers are often Democrats and why their offspring are born as Democrats. Democrats usually have platforms that include protection of unions, government support of the "poor," and more "rights" for women, minorities, and people with mixed gender.

Comparison of the 2008 Republican and Democrat Parties

Unfortunately, neither political party will define themselves. If you ask a leader in either party "What is a Democrat (or Republican)? They will not directly answer. They will give you the usual political doublespeak because they do not want to alienate any registered voter. Party leaders have growth-in-size and power as their assumed party job. They are differentiated however on their stances on issues. In 2008, the issue differences between Republicans and Democrats are shown below:

Republican Party	Democratic Party
Want less government	Want more government
Keep wages constant	Want higher minimum wage
Employers vote Republican	Minimum wage employees vote Democratic
Pro life	Pro choice
Pro gun	Ban guns
Oppose gay marriage	Pro gay/lesbian marriage
Pro tax cut	More taxes
No affirmative action	Pro affirmative action
Strong military	Military only to repel invasions
Strong global trade	Protectionism
Strong economy	Protectionism
Protestant	Catholic & Jewish
Against welfare	Pro welfare
Pro states rights	More federal control
Pro business	Tax hell out of business
Pro building wealth	Tax wealth from successful people
Less union control	Pro union growth
Pro death penalty	Anti death penalty

This list suggests that the two parties are distinguished by those wanting limited government and those wanting the government to take care of them from cradle to grave (Democrats).

This list is not the determining factor on the formation of America's two citizen groupings; it is people's perception of which group will best provide their welfare that determine which party they support. We are back to the basic motivations of mankind – freedom from pain and a desire for pleasure. Some people believe that less government will promote their personal welfare (freedom from pain of unemployment and the pleasures produced by disposable income); some people believe that a big government and lots of government programs can best promote their personal welfare. Thus, we have two parties because about half of the people feel that lots of government will give them life, happiness, and possessions, and half of the people believe that less government is the path to life, happiness, and possessions. The people in the splinter parties are too stubborn to admit that their pursuit of life, happiness, and possessions is not aided by participation in powerless political parties. They will die with their righteousness without making any progress toward a better democracy.

Strengths of America's Two-party System

Many countries that have a parliamentary democracy have many parties (Poland had 200 at one point) and to organize a government, they must form coalitions. These coalitions are fragile and governments can collapse at an event that shakes a coalition. It could be an event as minor as someone not being invited to a cocktail party. With many parties there is likely to be more warring. Each party wants the leadership position. Thus, having only two major parties creates a more stable government.

Having only two major parties simplifies election decisions for citizens. Americans are often asked to vote for 10 to 20 offices on a single ballot. If there were candidates for all 20 offices from 20 parties, we would have a hard time being a thoughtful, informed voter. It is often difficult to find out who is running for office from just two parties when we must vote on so many positions.

A good government is a simple government. If America had 20 political parties of importance, it would make our elections more complicated than they are. We have a hard time conducting valid elections – counting votes, etc. with two major parties. With 20 parties, the election process could become so complicated that nobody would vote. We have a participation problem now. It would be worse if we further complicated elections with more parties on each ballot. The campaigning would also be much more complicated and annoying (turn off) to potential voters. Having two parties simplifies the system and most citizens can force-fit themselves into one of our two parties.

Weaknesses in America's Two-party System

Your vote in almost any election in America means nothing unless it goes to candidates from either the Republican or Democratic Party. Needless to say, these parties do not fit the bill for many voters. We suggested that they have fundamental differences such as:

> Democrats – for big government
> Republicans – against big government
> Independents – do not participate in America's democracy

In the reality of the situation, in 2008, both major parties are probably so corrupt that they do not represent voter preferences or philosophies, but rather, they exist to provide elected jobs to party leaders and patronage jobs to fund raisers and campaign aids. I cannot speak for either party, but in my 40 plus years as a committee person, I have witnessed the change from a committee composed mostly of working people interested in participating in government to a committee run in secret by elected officials, and with a membership comprised of public employees who work for the elected officials. In my city, the party I belong to meets in city hall. The mayor calls all plays and I usually am the only person at committee meetings who does not work for the city. The mayor decides on all candidates for office. There are no candidates from the floor, no presentations – everything is decided in secret by the party's executive committee.

The county convention to select county office candidates is the same way. Everything is predetermined; we used to spend hours caucusing and voting at these conventions. Last year's was over in about 40 minutes. People were called up to make nominations, seconding speeches were previous prepared, and all the judgeships and elected office candidates were finalized in minutes.

So this is our dilemma. We must use the two parties because they are the only ones with the organization and funding to put forth serious candidates, but it is likely that those candidates are tainted; they are not the best candidates, but may only be cronies, relatives, or suck-ups who cannot really do the job that they are running for. In addition, there seems to be unnecessary acrimony between the various political parties. They view each other as mortal enemies instead of concerned citizens all working for the common good with different priorities. Henry Adams, the son of John Quincy Adams, once called political parties "organized hate." What a shame that situation still exists.

Author's Commentary

Some suggestions on improving political parties are:

1. *The local Democratic and Republican parties need to be audited by election commissioners to ensure that they function in a manner to allow public participation.*

2. *All political committees need to ban membership by government employees. Parties need to be returned to ordinary citizens.*

3. *The Democratic and Republican parties need to develop and publicize their party's political philosophy for voters to review.*

4. *The two major parties need an audit system to review what local committees are doing and certify them or not.*

As always, improving our democracy requires buy-in and action on the part of elected officials. One thing that citizens can do on their own is pick a party. Research Republican and Democratic Party activities, elected officials, and candidates in an area and decide which party is the best fit for your philosophy and well-

*being. Do not be a non participant in our democracy, an
"Independent." You can always vote for any candidate,
Democratic or Republican, but "Independents" do nothing to
make the system work. They perceive that being an Independent
shows independence. It only shows a dereliction of your duty to
participate. Independents do not field candidates. They do not
do petitions. They do not have committee members. They do not
participate in running America.*

*Minor party Americans are the real independents. They
are participating, they offer candidates; they campaign. They
show spirit and passion for their cause. They are good
Americans. However, they are too weak to accomplish the
changes that America needs. Only change in the Republican or
Democratic parties will help.   To that end, we need consensus
bylaws that apply to all political parties in the US and the only
way to prevent the corruption like I witnessed in my party is to
ban public employees from holding office in the political
committees. In my city, the heads of both the Democratic and
Republican Committees are chosen by elected officials. This
creates incontrovertible conflict of interest. Each selects
candidates to further their political careers not to present the
country's best to its leaders. Also, the Democratic and
Republican Committees need to make all of their meetings and
minutes open to the public. They need to establish a plan to
grow these committees and seek our best and brightest to run for
office. Maybe having SAT requirements would help. Many times
we are governed by people with insufficient intellect and
common sense. This must change if America is to survive as the
country that we perceive that it is.*

Questions

1.   What is a Democrat?
2.   What is a Republican?
3.   What is the problem with registering as an independent?

4.	What does it take for a party to field a candidate for election?
5.	What problems exist with minor parties?
6.	What is a party committee member?
7.	How are party leaders determined?
8.	What can be done to restore citizen participation in political parties?
9.	How are party philosophies determined?
10.	Who polices the operation of political parties?

Related Reading

1.	Weiss, David, What Democrats Talk About When They Talk About God: Religious Communication in the Democratic Party, 2010.

2.	Cronin, James E., Ross, George W., and Shoch, James, What's Left of the Left: Democrats and Social Democrats inChallenging Times, 2011.

3.	Frank, Bainez, What's Wrong With Democrats and How to Fix It, 1992.

4.	McCormick, Terri, What Sex is a Republican, 2010.

5.	Peterson, Peter G., Running on Empty: How the Democratic and Republican Parties are Bankrupting Our Future and What Americans Can do About it, 2005.

6.	Cain, Herman, They Think You're Stupid: Why Democrats Lost Your Vote and What Republicans Must Do to Keep It, 2005.

Chapter 13

Becoming a Candidate for Office

America's democracy does not make it easy to run for public office. The Constitution spells out major elected offices: President, Vice President, and members of Congress, but does not have guidelines for electing Americans to the plethora of elected offices that exist at the town, county, state, and federal levels. Over the years, federal, state, and counties (even towns and villages) have extablished laws governing election to public office. These must be complied with in order to run for elected office. They cover residency, petition requirements, timing – all sorts of details that must be complied with. Election statutes can be challenged in courts. For example, as this was being written, one of the most powerful politicians in America, the former Chief of Staff of the sitting president has been barred from running for the position of Mayor of Chicago, because for the past year, he was in D.C. working for the President. He is challenging the Chicago Election Commission decision in a state court. As most Americans recall, President George W. Bush became president because of a favorable Supreme Court decision on counting of ballots. So we have many laws to deal with in running for office. However, besides these laws, candidates need a campaign committee, party endorsement, or primary win to run. This chapter will discuss these issues.

Making the Decision

Unquestionably, the hardest part of running for elected office is making the decision. If the office is a full time position, your decision may affect your livelihood. If you have a job that does not allow sufficient time to run a campaign, you will have to quit your job or take a leave and then gamble on winning the election. This situation probably limits the aspirations of many

Americans who feel in their hearts that they can contribute to our democracy and the common good. Taking a leave to run for office is decidedly easy for people working in the public sector. So candidates from the private sector are at a disadvantage from the start.

If you are considering a run for a part-time office like city council, alderman, etc., you may not jeopardize your livelihood by deciding to run for elected office, but you are setting yourself up for scrutiny. Scrutiny will come from others in your party, your acquaintances, your neighbors, and the media. If there is something that you do not wish others to know about, then you may not want to run. Somebody will find what you are keeping secret and make it not secret. You will need to become familiar with the constituency of the office that you seek. Each level of government has a different constituency. There is a congressional district that contains several hundred thousand constituents. Then there may be a smaller state senate or assembly district, then a different county legislative district, then possibly a town election district and finally, there may be a city or town ward with yet again a different constituency. You must get the appropriate map from the election commissioner and learn who and how many citizens you will have to convince to vote for you.

Finally, there is a toll on your family. Running for office takes a great deal of your personal time. Getting elected usually takes more. Do you want to "short-change" your family? You will be tied up on weekends and evenings. If you are considering running for office, you must give serious consideration to the personal, family, and financial aspects of your decision.

Building a Campaign Team

It is very difficult to run for any office with no supporters. If you have none, you may consider this a show stopper. Do not run. However, if you have at least one other person (for example, a spouse) you have a campaign team. You will need a campaign "team" to at least second your nomination at a party nominating convention. You will need a campaign chair to handle (and raise) your campaign funds. Your chair also must take care of your pig roast and petition needs. Needless to say, your supporters must really believe in you. They must feel that you will make America and their lives better if you get elected to public office. So a campaign committee with as many loyalists as possible is essential.

Getting a Party Nomination

Becoming your party's candidate for a particular office is the best option for running for elected office. With the nomination comes petition help, campaign help, possibly funds, and most important, you are the designated candidate for all of the people registered in you party in your district or area in which you are running. What it takes to get the party's nomination varies with the individual town, city, state, etc. committees. At the grass roots level – the local committee you start the process if running for nomination when the party secretary informs the committee that we are seeking candidates for these offices: xxxx, for the Fall 2011 elections. You inform the secretary that you want the party's designation as their candidate. If the secretary gets more than one candidate for each office, than the committee uses some process to select the committee's choice from the six or whatever candidates. Sometimes a screening committee will interview the candidates and present their opinion of the best. Sometimes the candidates are given an opportunity to speak to the committee and committee members vote on the "best" candidate. If you get the nomination, you can start your campaign against the other party opponents. If you do not get the nomination, you can fade back into ordinary committee membership or you can run a primary.

Conducting a Primary

Primaries are government sanctioned and financed elections held significantly (months) before general elections to let voters with a particular party decide on who the party candidate will be. To force a primary, you need to meet the 5% signature requirement. If your election district has 1,000 registered party members, you will need to garner 50 signatures to force a primary. Of course, as the size of the area gets larger, you may need 10,000 signatures. The designated party candidate will already have the necessary petition signatures. His or her name will be on the petitions that are circulated in June for November elections. The primary will be in August or September – at least a month before the election. Rich people can hire others to get petitions signed. Not-rich people need to rely on their campaign staff and usually you only have 30 days to get the required number of signatures. Thus, primaries are not that easy to do. Getting the party's nomination is the preferred path.

Getting Elected

In America it is essential to get your name recognized. Americans do not vote for a name that they see for the first time on a paper ballot. If they have seen or heard your opponent's name and not yours, he or she gets the vote. Of course, this is wrong. American citizens who take their democracy seriously will take the time to research issues, candidates for office, and pray over their selection. They will choose the person with the best qualifications as gleaned from their research. Unfortunately, not all Americans research issues and candidates for all offices. So as a candidate, you must get your name to be recognized; you must try to give a voter a reason to vote for you; and you must get the voter to vote. All of these things take advertising dollars, personal contacts, and any marketing technique that you can get your hands on.

Strengths of America's Election System

We have a very rigorous election system. There are procedures for everything. The political parties pick their candidates at a designated time, the petitions are circulated a designated time, primaries are held at a designated time, elections are held at a designated time, and ballots are counted in a designated way. Nothing is left to chance. This thoroughness on the part of election commissioners and their staff makes the electoral process of our democracy run smoothly.

The campaign procedures are equally thorough. Each political party has procedures and times designated for fund raisers, for lawn signs, for TV advertisements, etc. The town, city or village political party committees have seasoned politicians who can mentor newcomers. There are many details that must be mastered to make our system work and the "teachers" are in the political committees. We have the expertise to make elections run smoothly.

Weakness of America's Election System

The most significant weakness of America's system for running for elected office is that the "procedure" requires such an investment of time and money that many ordinary working people cannot afford either and thus do not run for office even though he or she may be a brilliant leader.

Most elected officials in America are "lifers". They have not held any other job in their adult life other than elected official/public employee. Most judges become assistant district attorneys or law clerks right out of law school. They never really worked as a lawyer. All of the US Presidents for the past 60 years spent their entire life in politics/public service. Most governors worked their way up from mayoral positions or the like.

Our system is such that the diversity of its citizenry is not reflected in government. Factory workers, engineers, farmers, masons, doctors are not represented. This is a serious weakness.

Author's Commentary

However difficult it may be for your personal life, the reward of knowing that you are contributing to America's democracy makes it all worthwhile. That is if you are running because of an honest belief that you have a better idea and you are not running for the power and money. Voters sense your intentions. One of the reasons why Ronald Regan was the most revered president over the part 60 years is that he already had more power and money than any person needs before he sought the presidency. He only ran to help his country.

So if you have impeccable credentials, the appropriate education and training, and a love of your country, please run for office at any level. America needs ordinary people as opposed to career politicians. We cannot sustain our democracy without citizens coming forward to run for elected office.

Questions

1.   How do you know the constituency for a given elected office?
2.   Who determines constituencies for an office?
3.   How do you get nominated as a party's candidate for an office?
4.   What are the petition requirements for a primary?
5.   When is a primary necessary?
6.   How does a person fund a candidacy for office?
7.   When are primaries held?
8.   Who get petitions signed?
9.   Where does a candidate get the necessary petitions?
10.   What must a person do to get his or her party's nomination for a particular office?

Related Reading

1.   Faircheux, Ron, <u>Running for Office: The Strategies, Techniques, and Messages Modern Candidates Need to Win Elections</u>, 2002.

2.   MacNamara, Michael, <u>The political Campaign Desk Reference: A Guide for Campaign Managers and Candidates Running for Office</u>, 2008.

3.   Fale, Mary Anne, Friedman, Jane, and VanderWal, Todd, <u>Running for Office – Getting Yourself Elected to the Career You Really Want</u>, 2009

4.   Greg, Lawrence, <u>How to Win a Local Election</u>, 2007.

5.   DeCapua, Sarah, <u>Running for Public Office</u>, 2002.

Chapter 14

The Role of Every American in Our Democracy

A democracy, by definition, is a form of government where the citizenry participates in running the government. How many Americans currently feel that they have input into running America? Most of us are on the receiving end of countless laws, mandates, fees, and taxes and we do not want most of them. How did we get into this situation? We ceded control of the country, states, counties, and towns to professional politicians – people whose only jobs have been various pubic employee jobs. Review your local elected officials. How many have other jobs? How many were factory workers, electricians, miners, checkout clerks? If there are none in your area, you do not have a participating democracy. This final chapter deals with ways that each and every one of us can do our part in maintaining America's democracy.

Question all Laws

Unfortunately many, if not most, laws that we have in America are based upon reactions to events which very often are one-time happenings. When a person walking across a street gets hit by a car and killed or severely injured, we will see a traffic control device at the spot soon afterward. America has hundreds of laws on the books as reaction to the terrorist attack on the World Trade Center. We have laws on the books as reactions to horses that may get out of control. In New York State, there is a law against elephant riding – apparently resulting from someone getting injured while attempting to ride an elephant at a circus or some such event.

One of the main objectives of this book is to get Americans with common sense and reason involved in politics so that we do not have frivolous laws that attack our freedoms. America needs people to question all laws, their impact on freedoms, their impact on economics, their impact on our environment, and if they are absolutely without any reasonable doubt necessary and their necessity will endure for as long as our democracy endures. We need legislators to question the current relevancy and benefit to the common good of every law and eliminate those that were reactions to isolated events.

Study Issues

In 2010, Americans were saturated with opinions (news) from media that was in your face wherever you were. All public meeting places like restaurants and waiting rooms had walls cluttered with TV's turned on to talk shows where they rehash the last 15 minutes of happenings every half hour. Smart phones serve up the same hash wherever you are. Then the e-mail providers rehash everything again. How can an American find out what is happening locally and worldwide without having it digested and expurgated by personalities? Printed newspapers may be all that America has left. They are dying because advertising is shifting to electronic devices, but the press is the only institution standing between democracy and tyranny. The first step that a dictator takes when seizing power is to take over the communications systems in a country: radio, TV, the press, and now, the internet.

An elected official may be stealing from the federal, state, county, town, or village treasury and if there is no unbiased third party (the press) to inform the citizens, he or she will keep doing it. The same thing is true about our liberties. They can be quietly taken away by incomprehensible (to us) legislation and we would never know until they are gone. We must have a free press to survive and citizens of America have the responsibility to study issues pertaining to our democracy so that they can speak out and act on issues not in keeping with freedom and the common good (and common sense, like the elephant ban).

Citizens must establish a position on every issue and fight for it in every way available. For example, this week a state senator in New York committed the most flagrant indiscretion (but not unlawful) possible and casually laughed it off to the electorate. The indiscretion clearly showed the electorate that he was not fit to serve in any public office and the outpouring of calls for resignation from the electorate resulted in his resignation. How wonderful. Speaking out against "bad things" is necessary and it can lead to improvements to our society as in this instance: one dirt bag senator gone.

Vote Without Fail

Any failings in America's democracy can be traced to the root cause of voter apathy. When citizens do not research issues and vote intelligently, we get stupid unnecessary laws (like no elephant riding), dirt bag public officials (state senator, etc.), we lose freedoms (like the 2010 health care boondoggle) our democracy suffers and we can be taxed into poverty as a nation. So many terrible things have happened to America because not enough people vote. Less than 50 percent of Americans vote in presidential elections. Local school board elections may be down to 10%. America has not been functioning as a true democracy because of our terrible voting performance.

Many people claim that their vote does not count. Of course it does. Each election anywhere in the US will probably have a race or proposition that wins or loses by a handful of votes – sometimes out of millions. Every vote matters. Every citizen has a duty based upon his or her citizenship to vote in every election at every level in their locality. Votes are the plasma that keeps a democracy alive.

Participate to the Extent of Your Time and Abilities

Every person has abilities that set them apart from all others. Some are good debaters; some are good thinkers; some

have good manual skills; some have good spelling skills, etc.
We all have gifts. Part of life is sharing of your gifts. If you
have a unique skill like chair caning, you have a duty based upon
your existence to do something with this ability, to share it, to
use it to please others, to capitalize on it. To let it die without
growth is to be a failure as a human being. We must use our
gifts; we must share them; we must use the ones that apply to
participate in our democracy, our common good. We must
always try to use our gifts to help others.

Many Americans rationalize their lack of participation in
our democracy to lack of time. Americans will have more time
on their hands than ever if they fail to devote time to our
democracy. We may never have a job. In 2010, America is
heading in the direction of no jobs in the private sector. We have
lost almost all manufacturing jobs; business jobs are on their way
to India and the Orient, and health jobs are next to be outsourced
to low-cost countries. So Americans will have lots of time on
their hands if they do not take the time to participate in the
running of their democracy.

Author's Commentary

*It is difficult to write about how America's democracy
works without pointing out the perceived weaknesses in our
democracy. Sorry. America really, really needs young people to
embrace their democracy and fix what is broken and make it
better. They need to make it like the Constitution intended; they
need to make elected officials accountable, ethical, honest, just,
and have common sense. They need to accept that nurturing
their democracy is a lifelong obligation. If this is done, they will
feel better about their lives and their lives will be much better
with freedom, jobs, and happiness.*